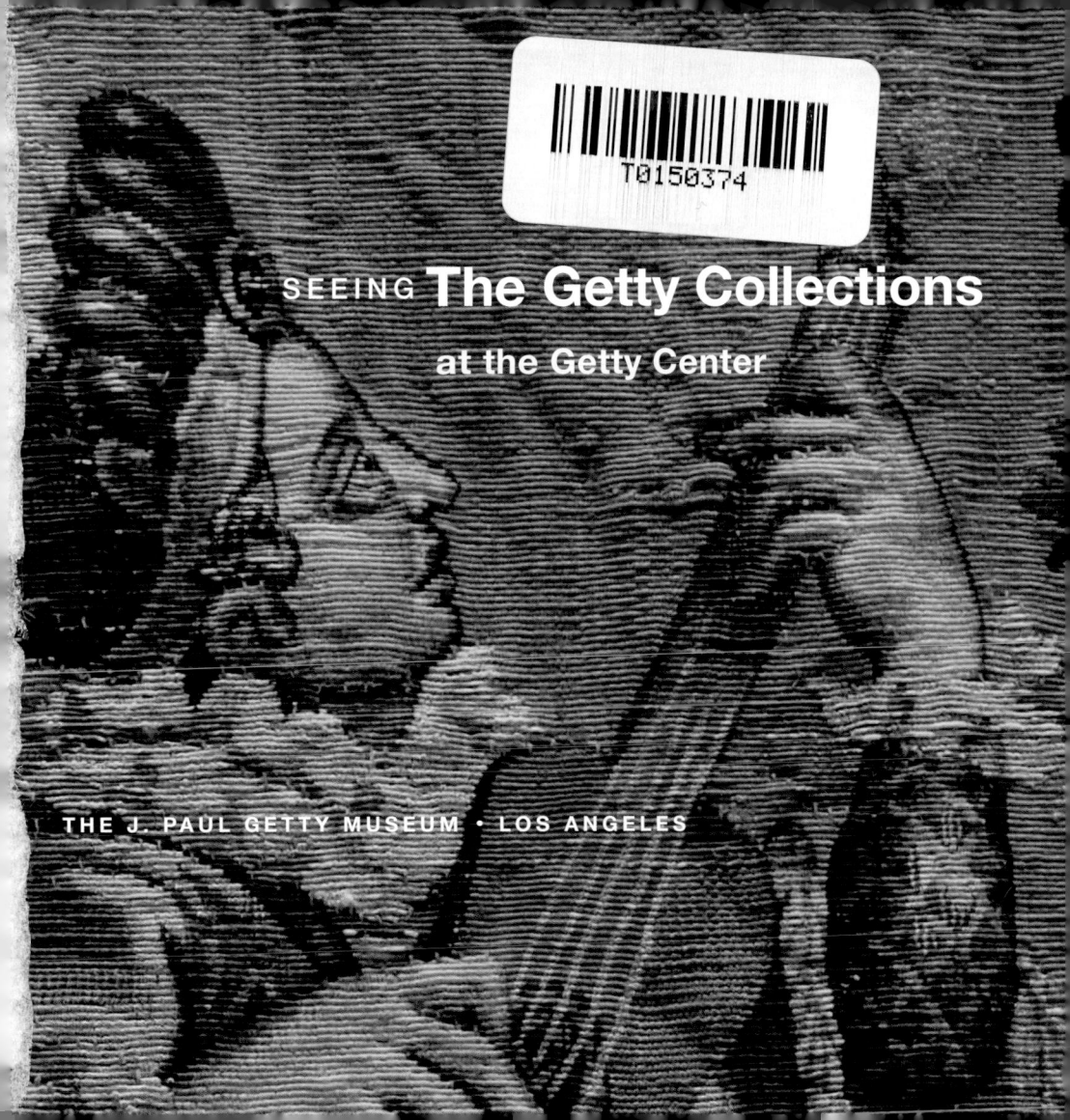

T0150374

# SEEING The Getty Collections

## at the Getty Center

THE J. PAUL GETTY MUSEUM • LOS ANGELES

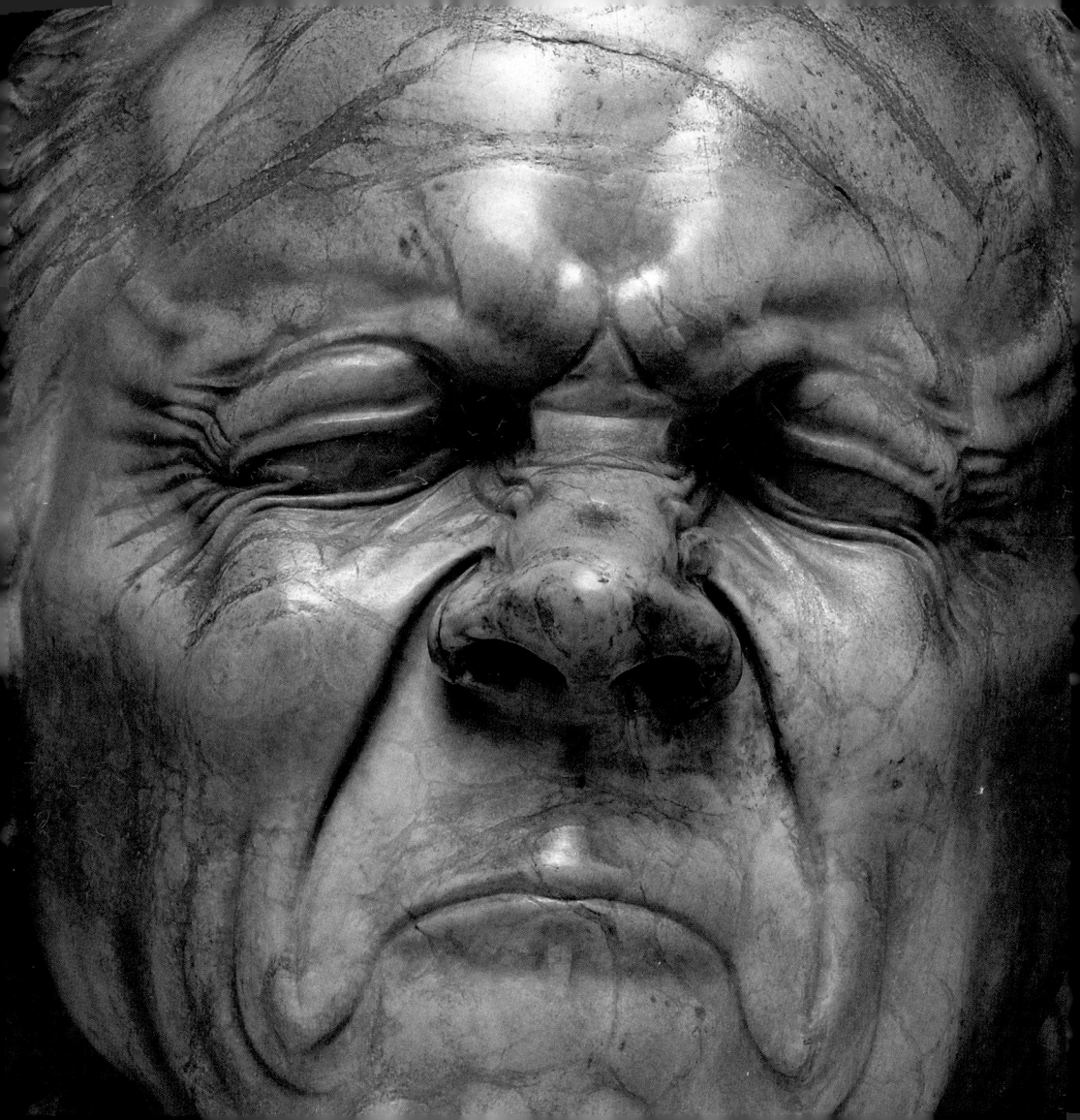

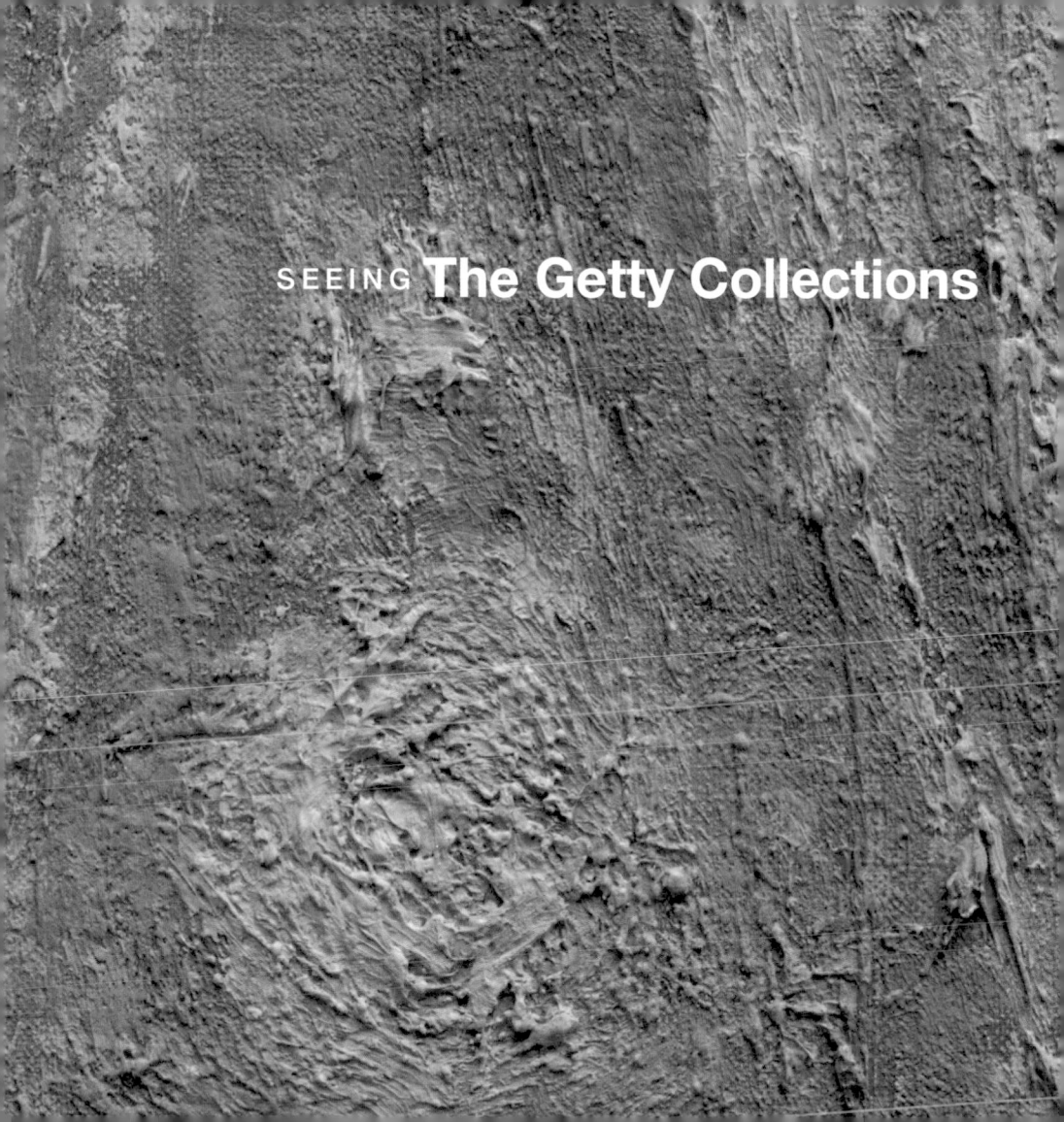

# SEEING The Getty Collections

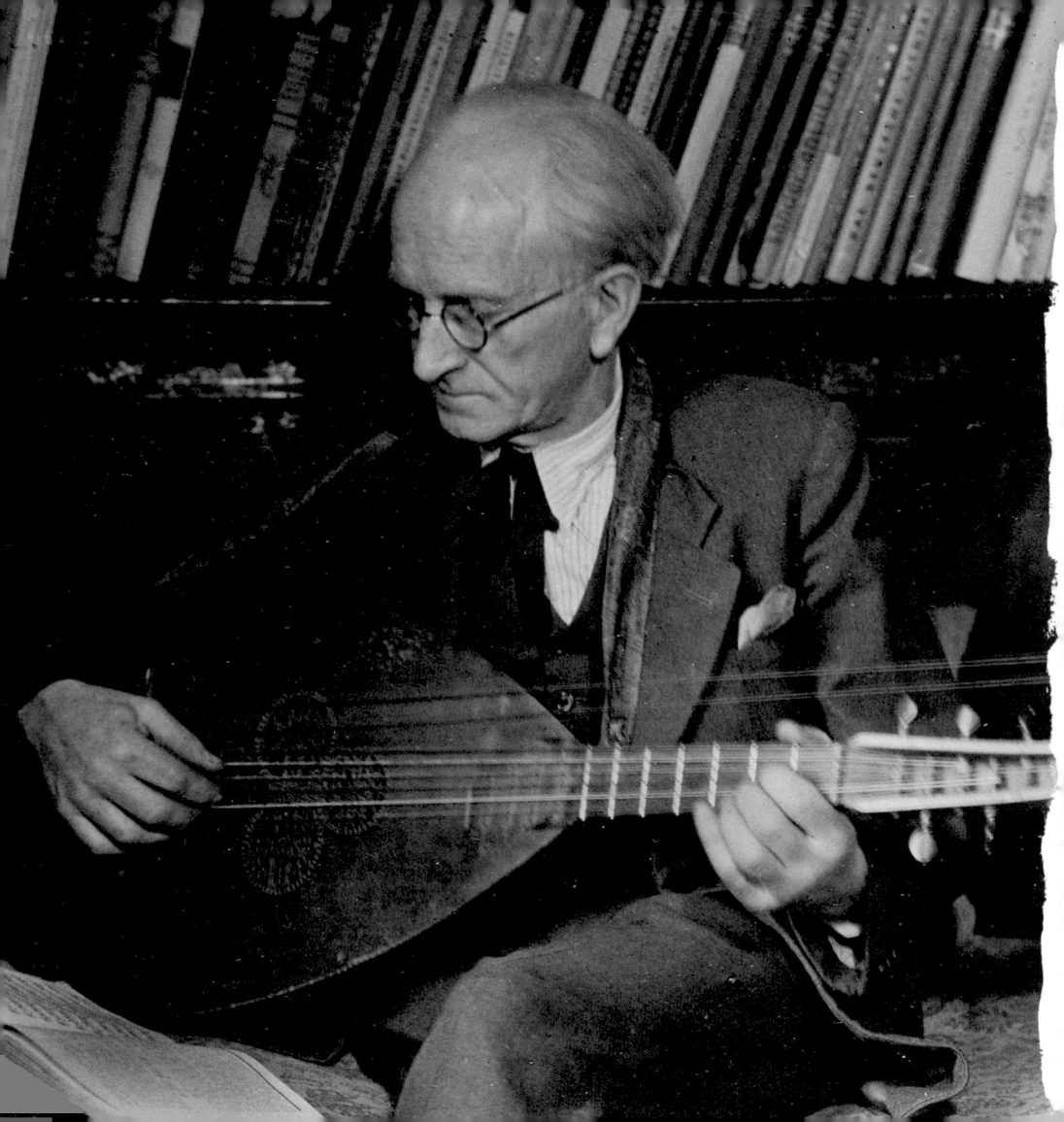

# FOREWORD

The experience of touring a museum is unique to every visitor. Each of us comes with our own expectations, memories, knowledge, tastes. Some of us come for a very focused purpose—to see a particular work we are professionally interested in or to see a special exhibition we have heard about and found intriguing—and some of us come simply to spend an hour or two in old, familiar galleries among works we have known for years or to wander amid a collection entirely new to us. And when we leave, we take our own particular impressions with us—memories of works, or even simply parts of works, that struck us as beautiful or odd or mysterious.

In this small book, we have tried to recreate the experience of visiting a museum, and the surprise and delight of discovering similarities among otherwise disparate works. In trying to capture what any of us might take away from a casual stroll through our collections, we have chosen to show portions of works that bear coincidental or perhaps purposeful relationships—in style or subject—to other works pictured next to them. Although we think the works chosen for this book are very fine indeed, we are not singling them out as "highlights." We simply chose those that caught the trained and eager eyes of our photographic staff or of the designer of this volume, Kurt Hauser, and that led them to see connections among the works that, in many cases, they themselves were noticing for the first time. All the works are described on the last pages of the book.

We hope you will enjoy leafing through this "virtual tour;" we hope that you will see a few works that are familiar to you and others that you would like to examine more closely. Most of all, we hope that this book entices you to visit the Getty, again and again.

David Bomford
Associate Director of Collections
The J. Paul Getty Museum

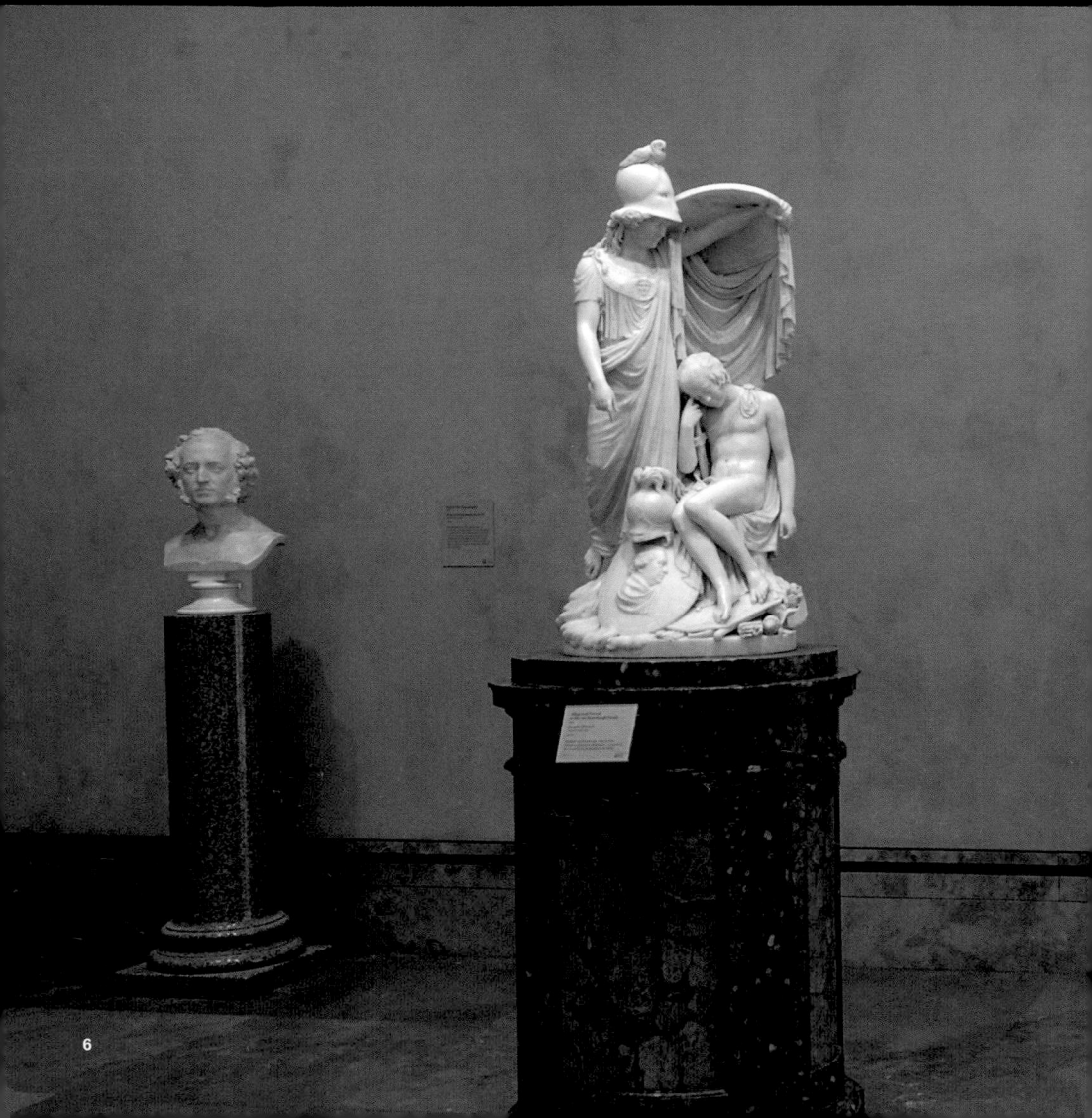

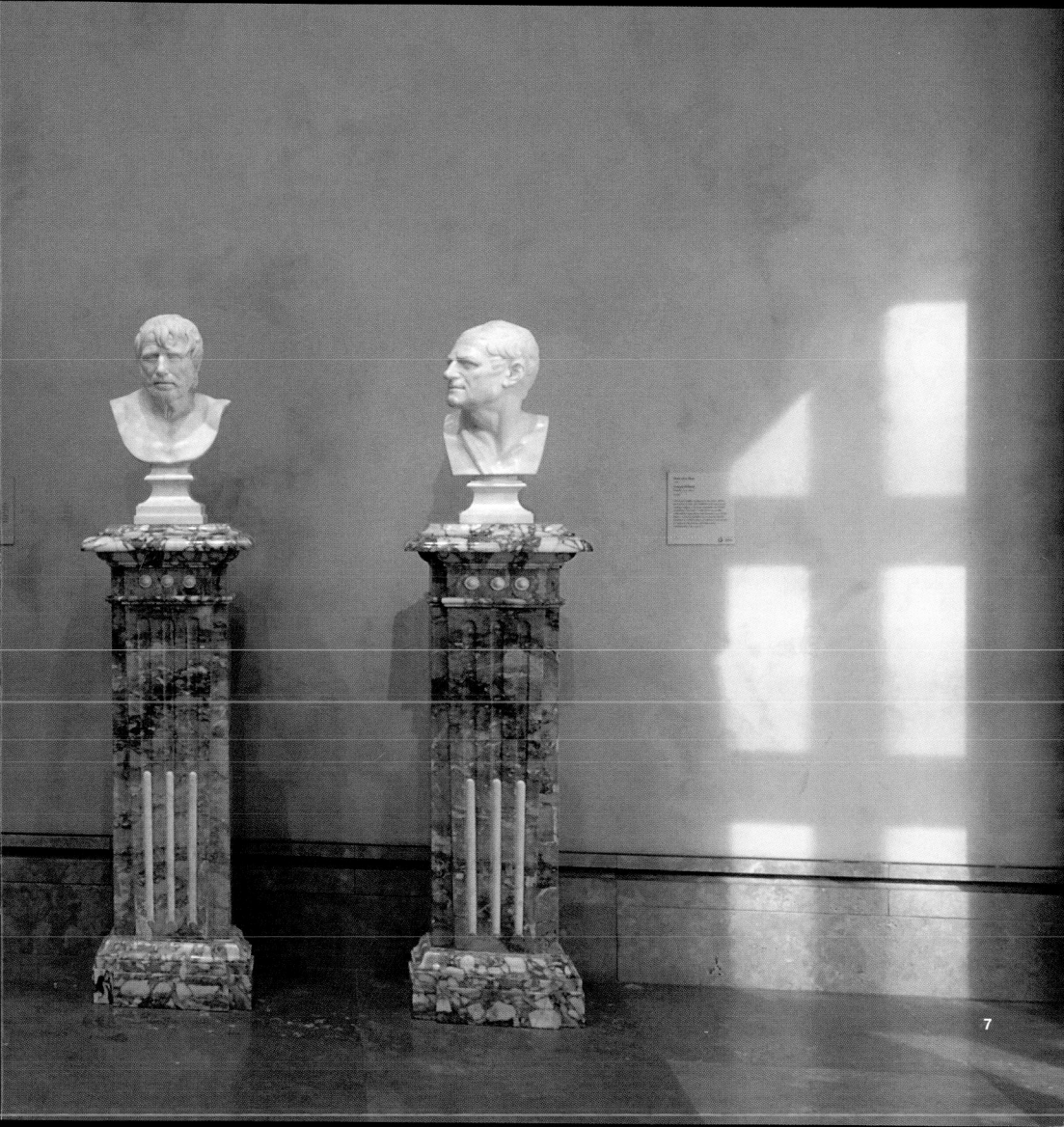

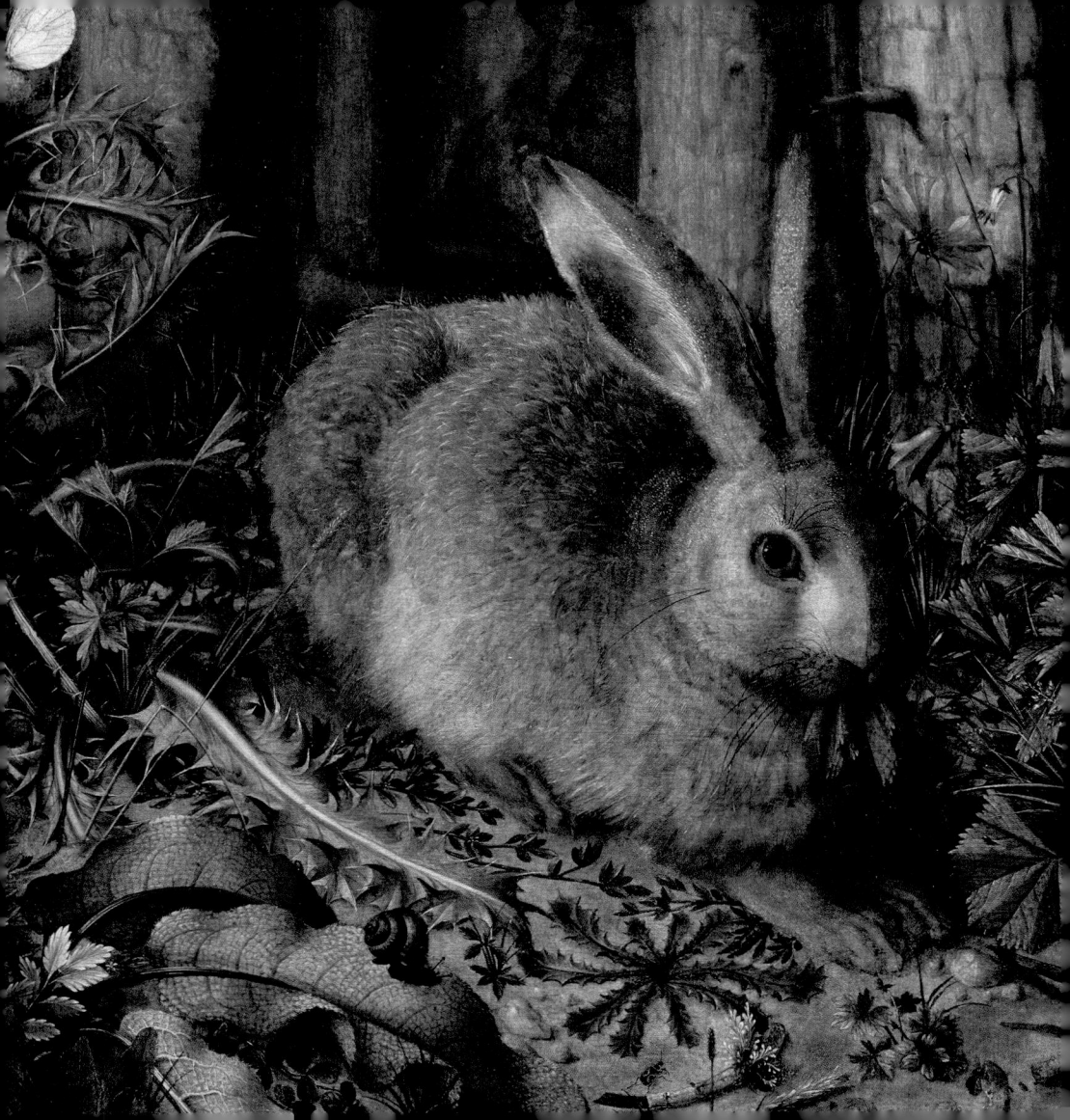

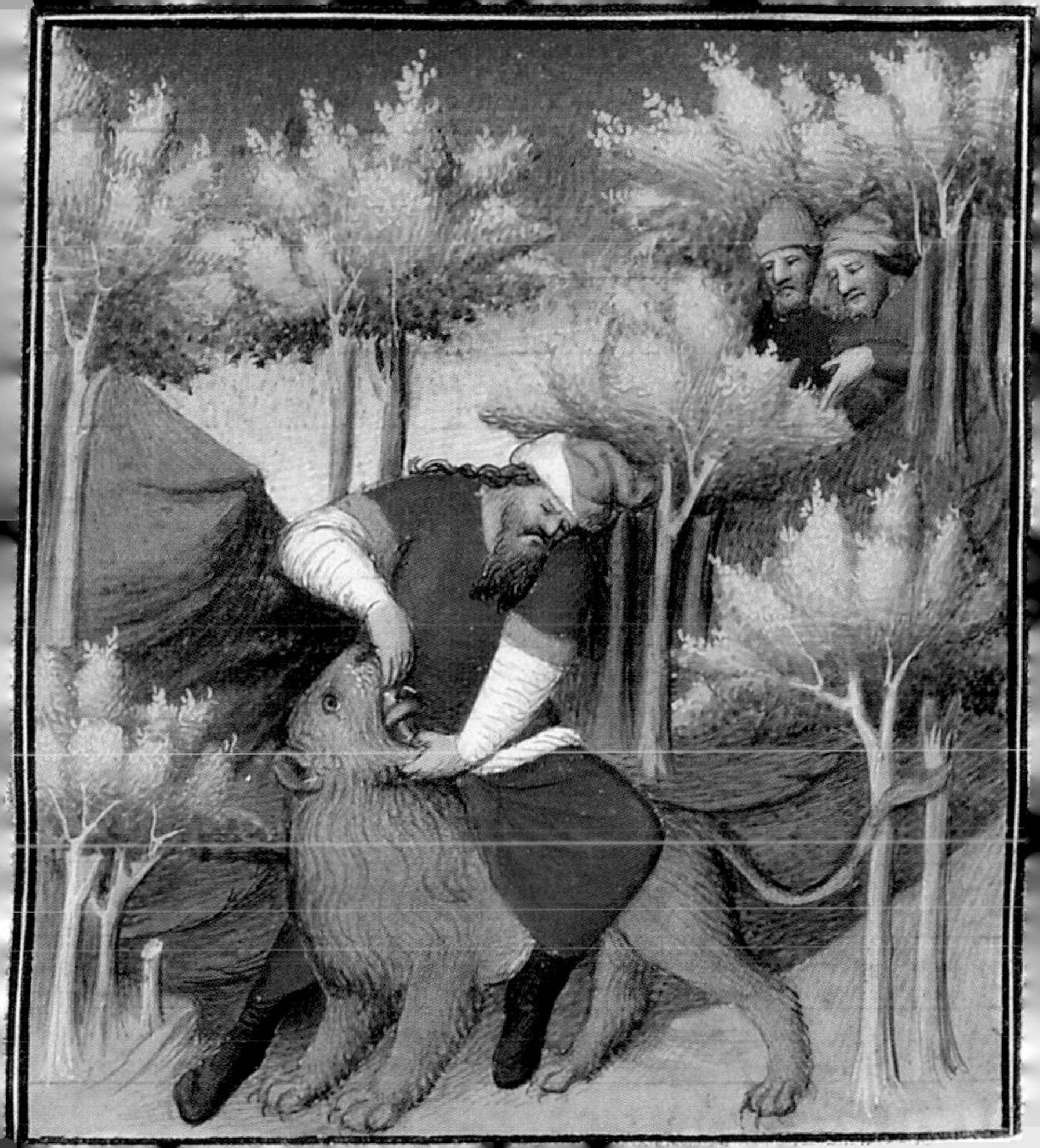

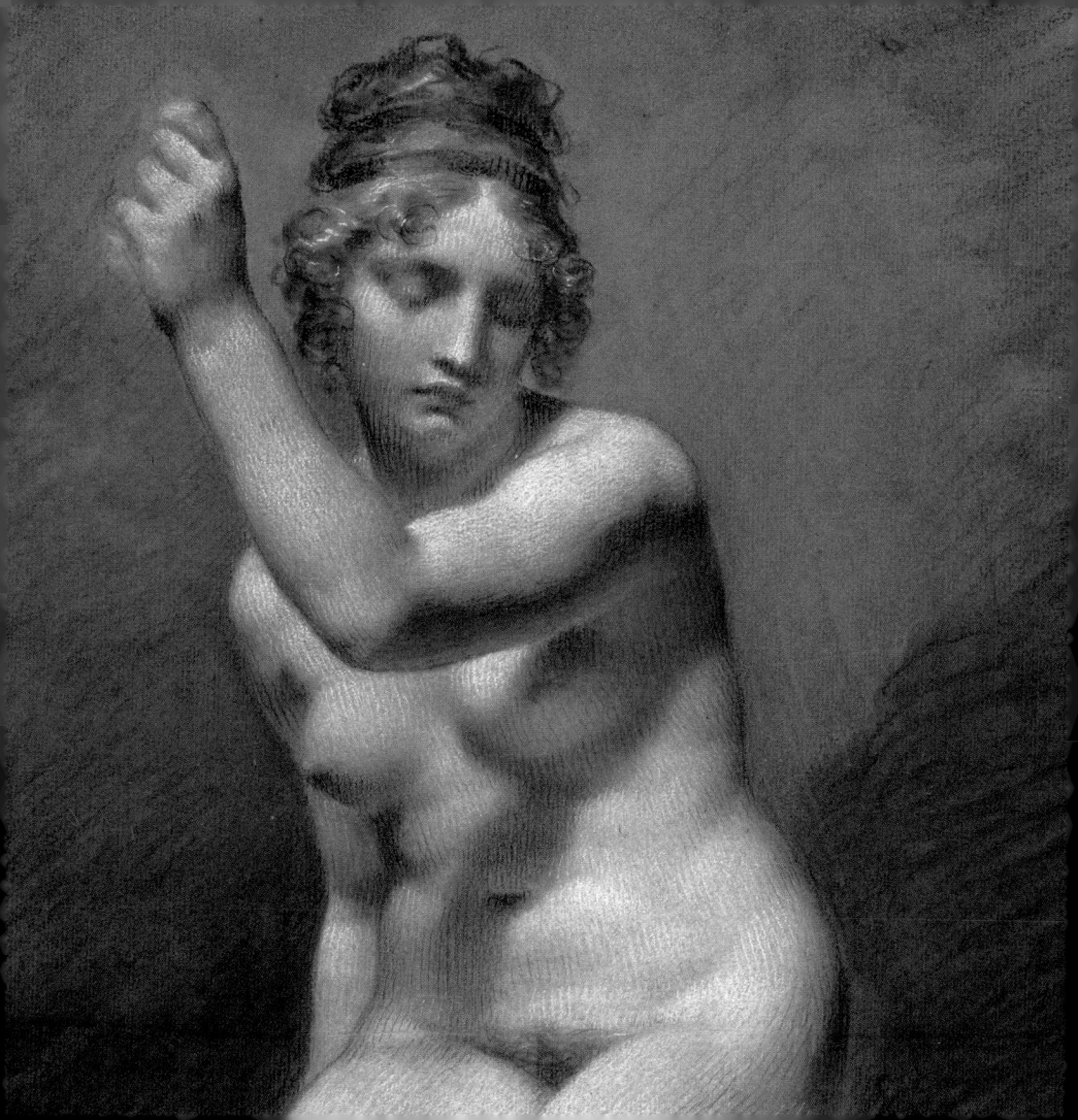

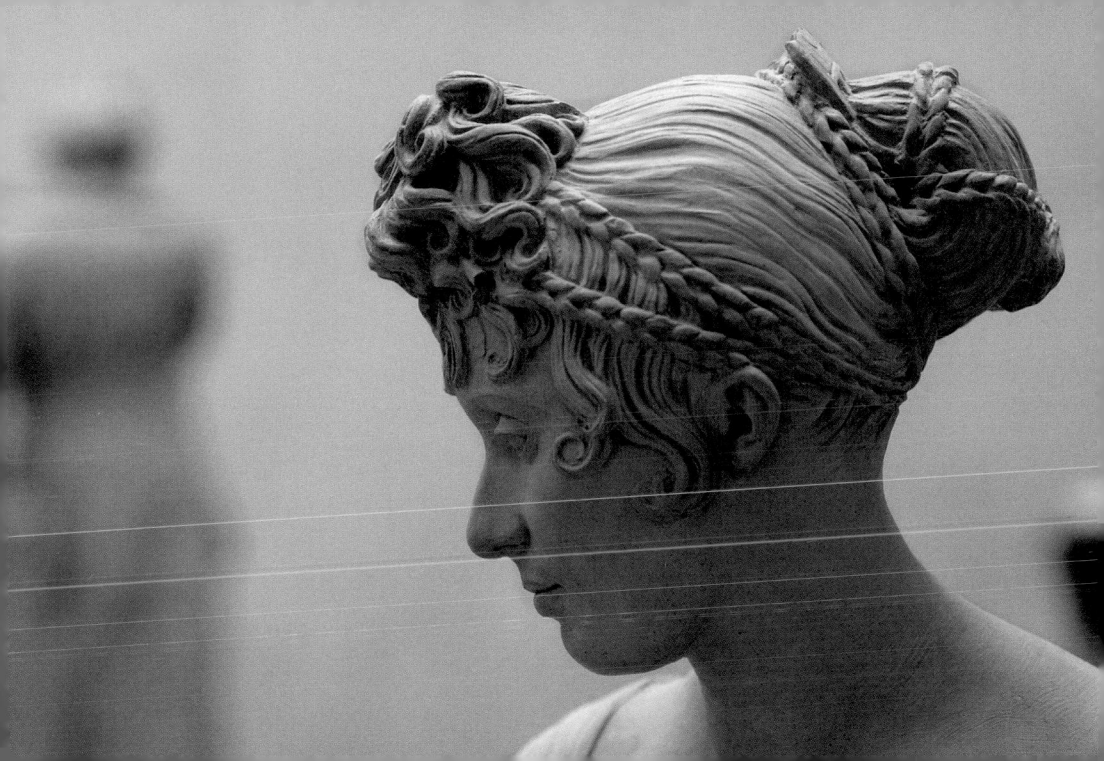

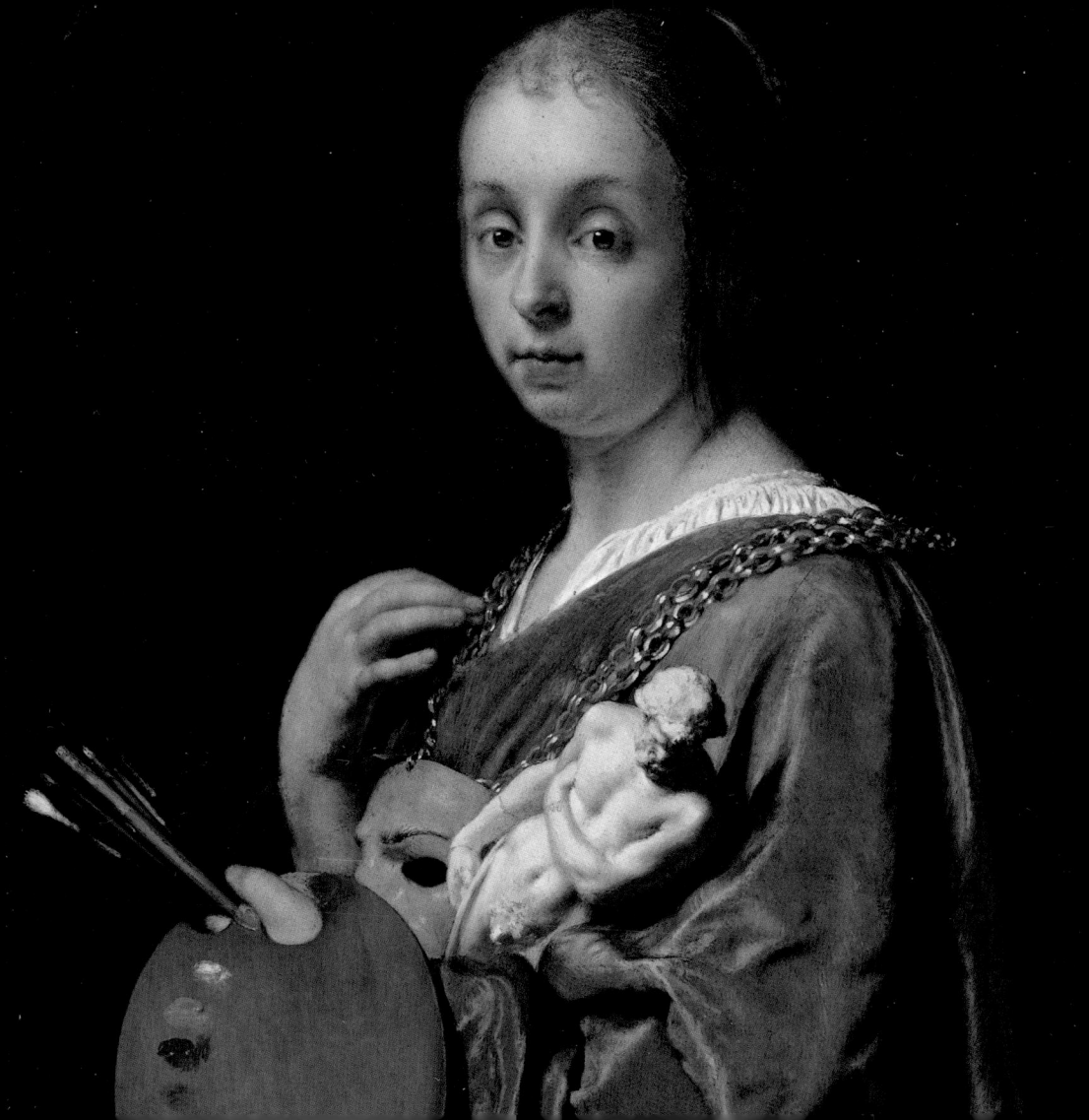

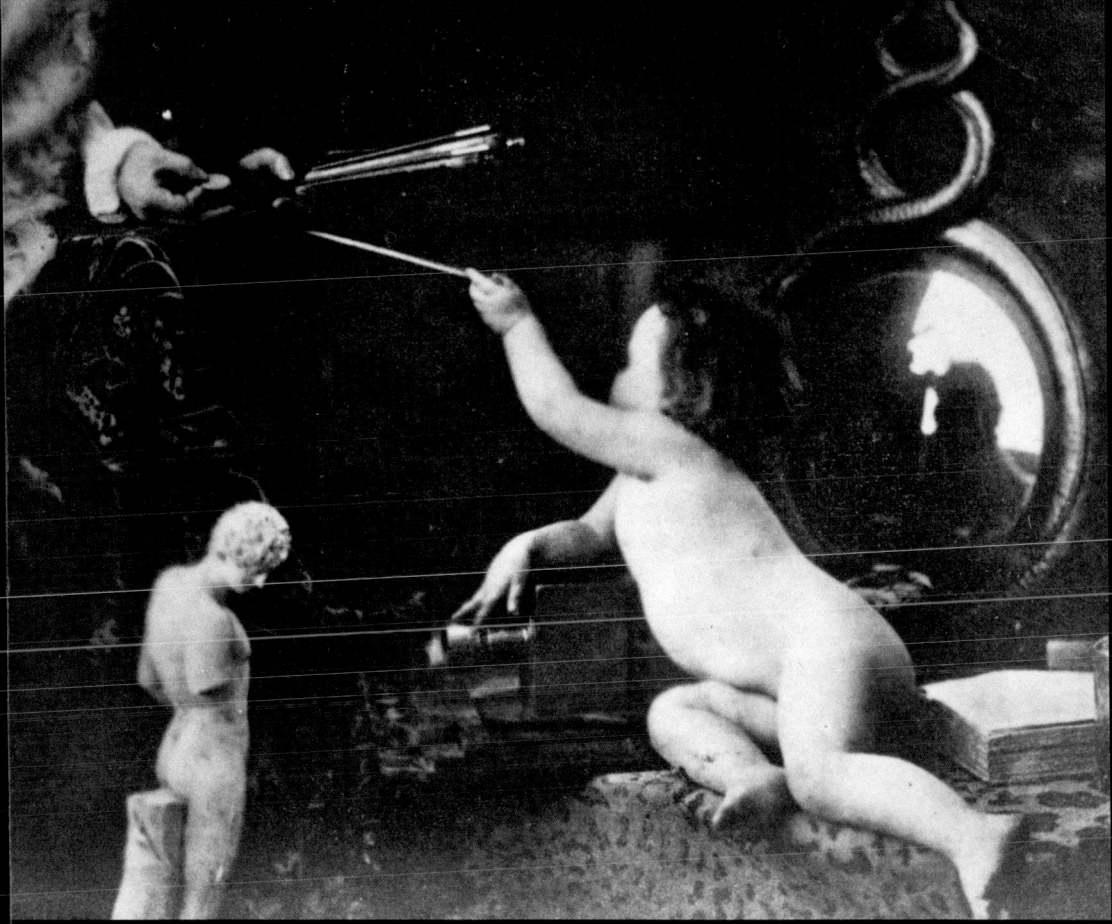

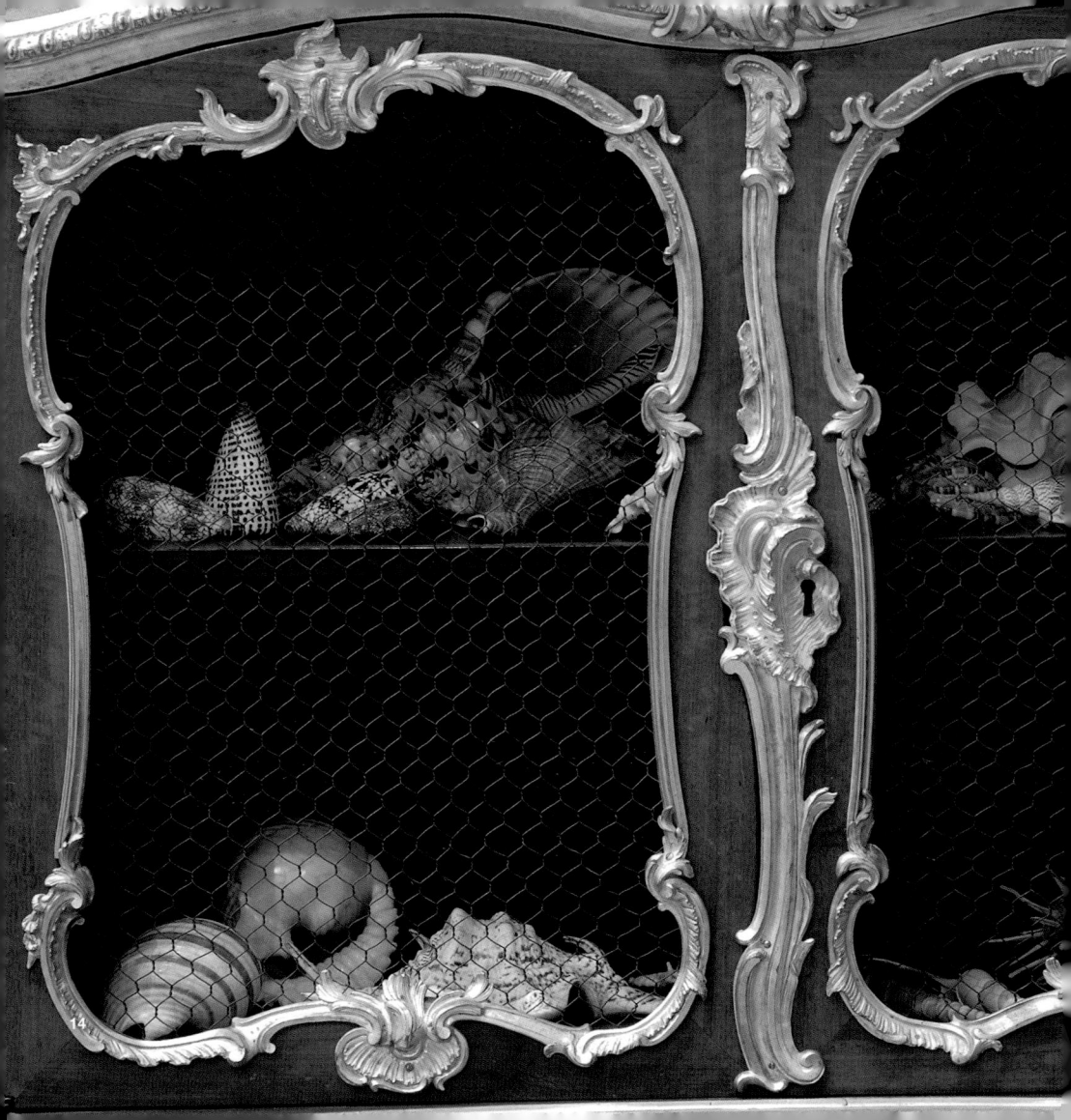

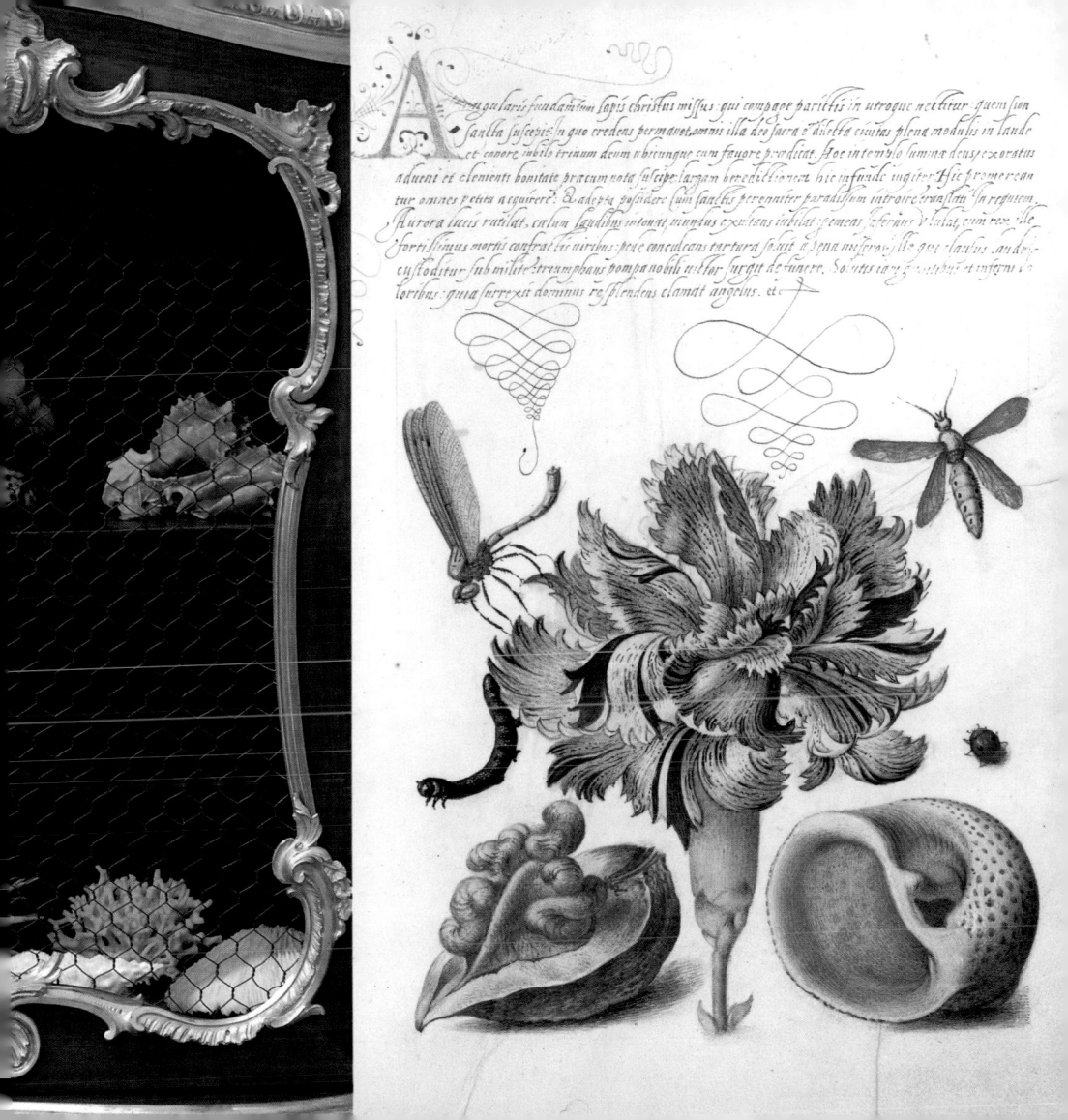
Angularis fundamentum sapis christus missus: qui compage parietis in utroque nectitur: quem sion
sancta suscepit: in quo credens permanet omnis illa dei sacra & dilecta civitas plena modulis in laude
et canore inebrio trinum deum vbicunque cum fauore prodicat. Hoc interuallo lumina deus exoratus
adueni et clementi bonitate pretium nota suscepe: largam hereditem non hic infunde ingitur: Hic promerean
tur omnes rem aequirere. Quadepta possidere cum sanctis perennitter paradisum introire transeunt. In regnum
Aurora lucis rutilat. cælum laudibus intonat. mundus exultans iubilat. gemens inferius dolet. cum rex ille
fortissimus mortis contrahet uiribus: pene euculcans tartarum saeuit a pena miserum. illo quo clausus antea
custoditur sub milite triumphans pompa nobili nitetur. surgit de tumere. Solutis enim gemitibus et inferni do
loribus: quia surrexit dominus resplendens clamat angelus. etc

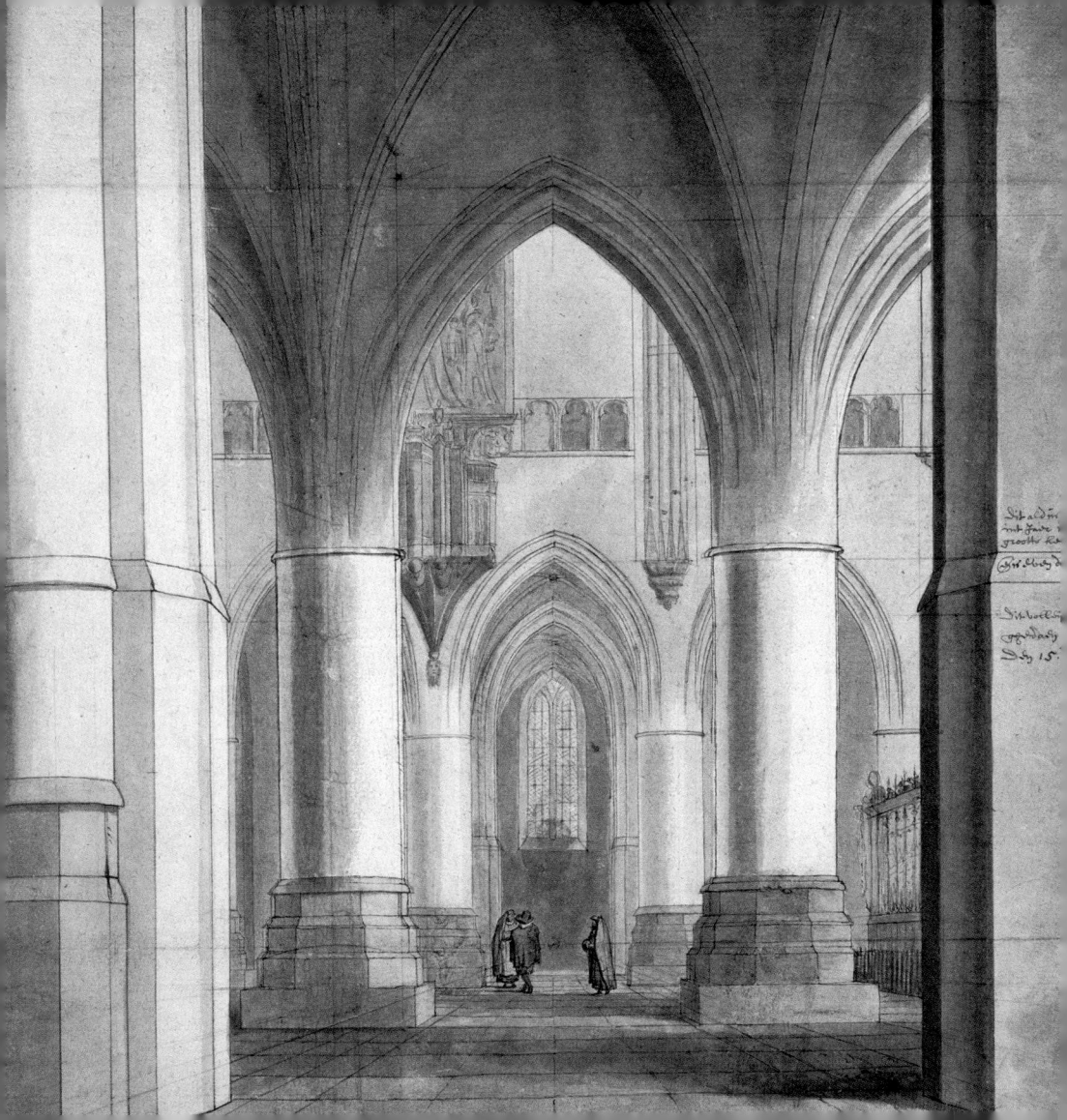

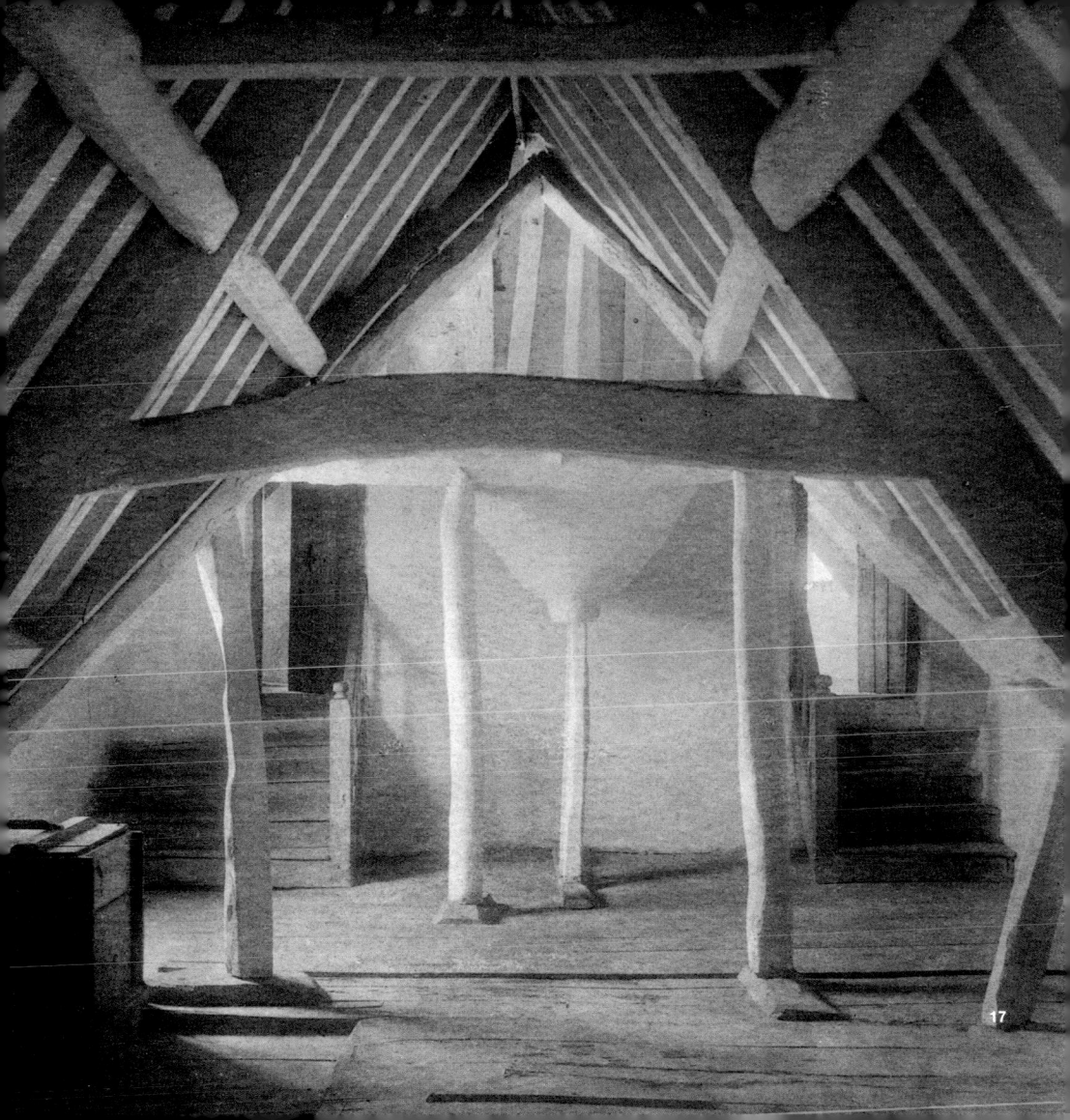

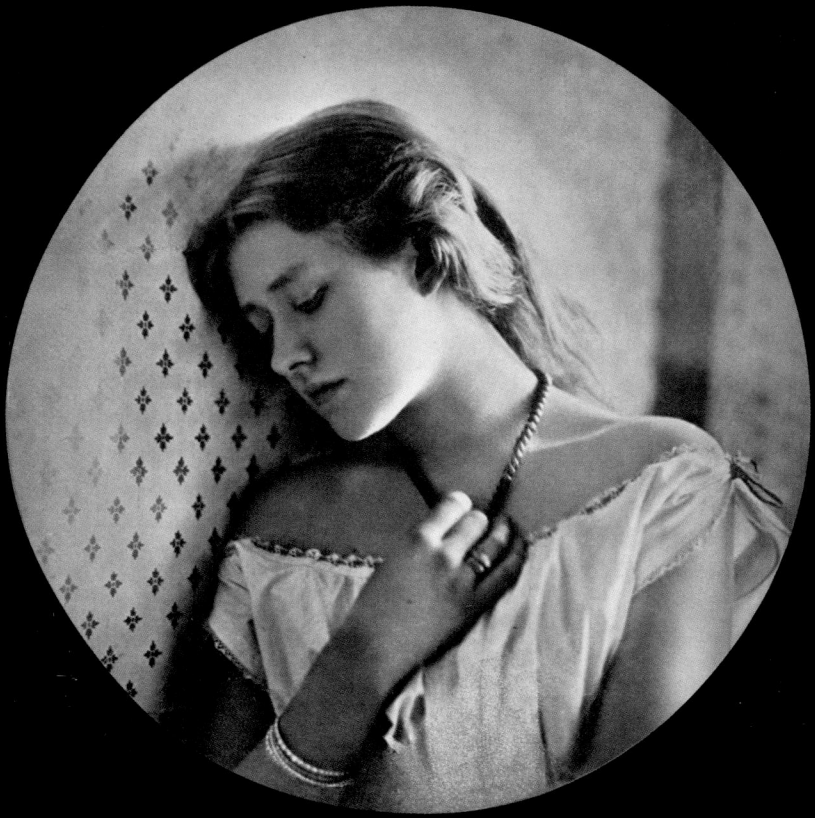

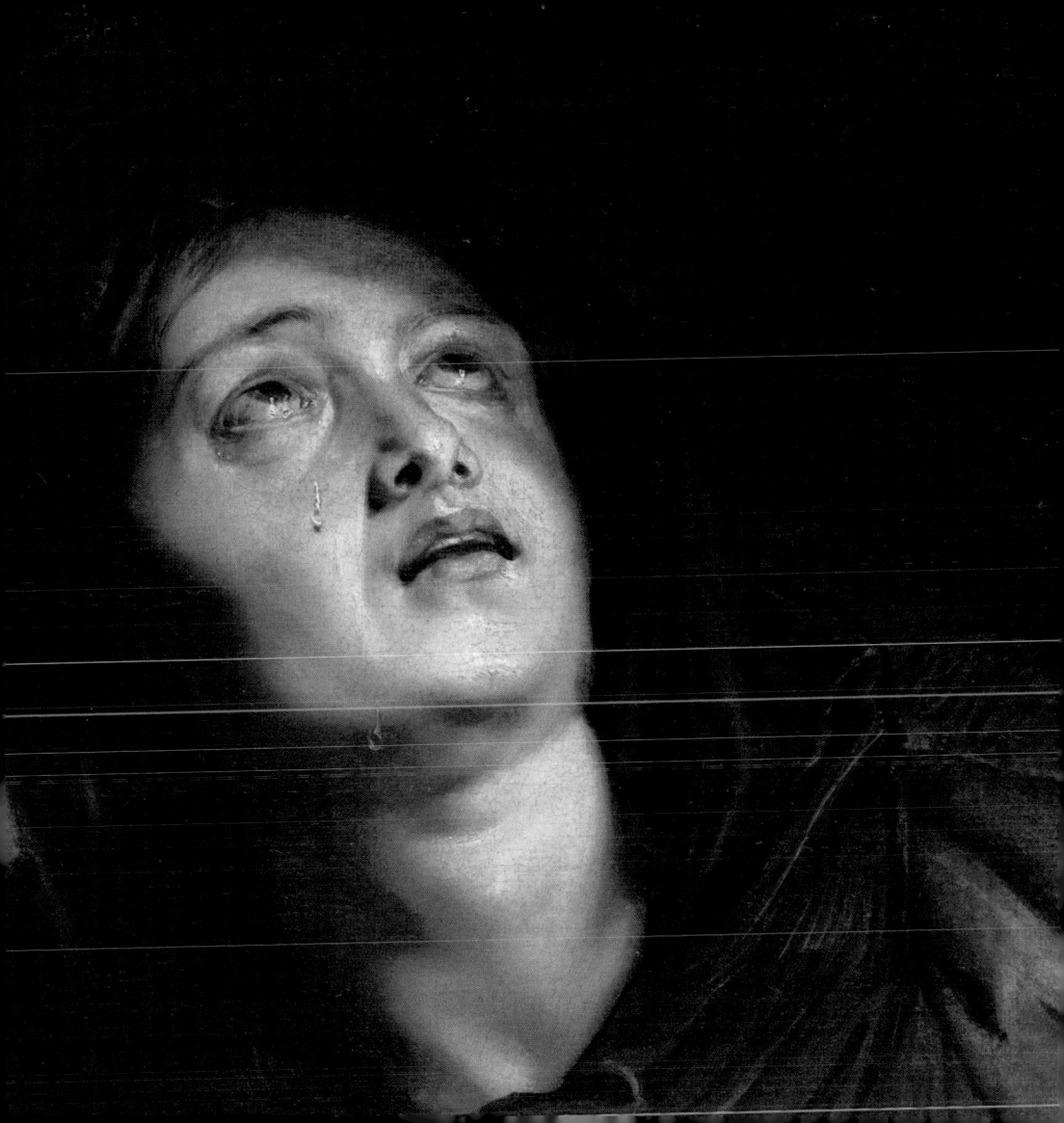

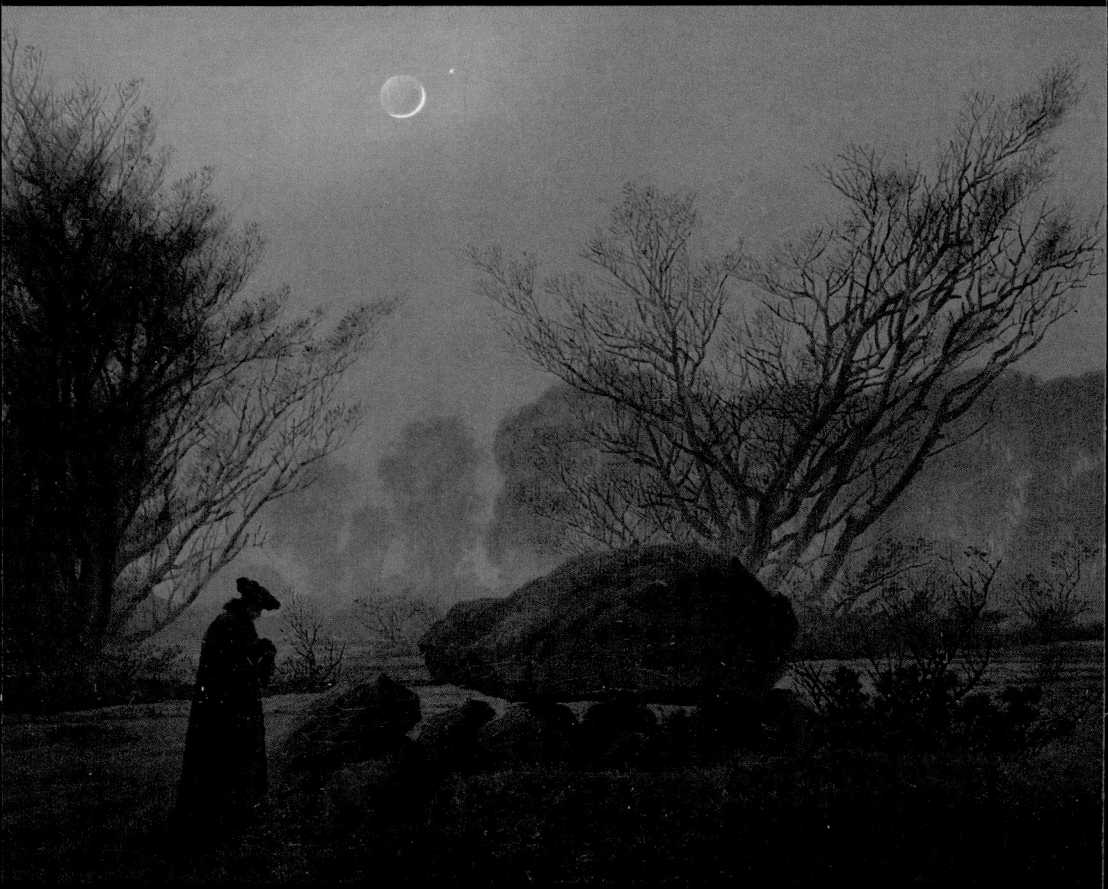

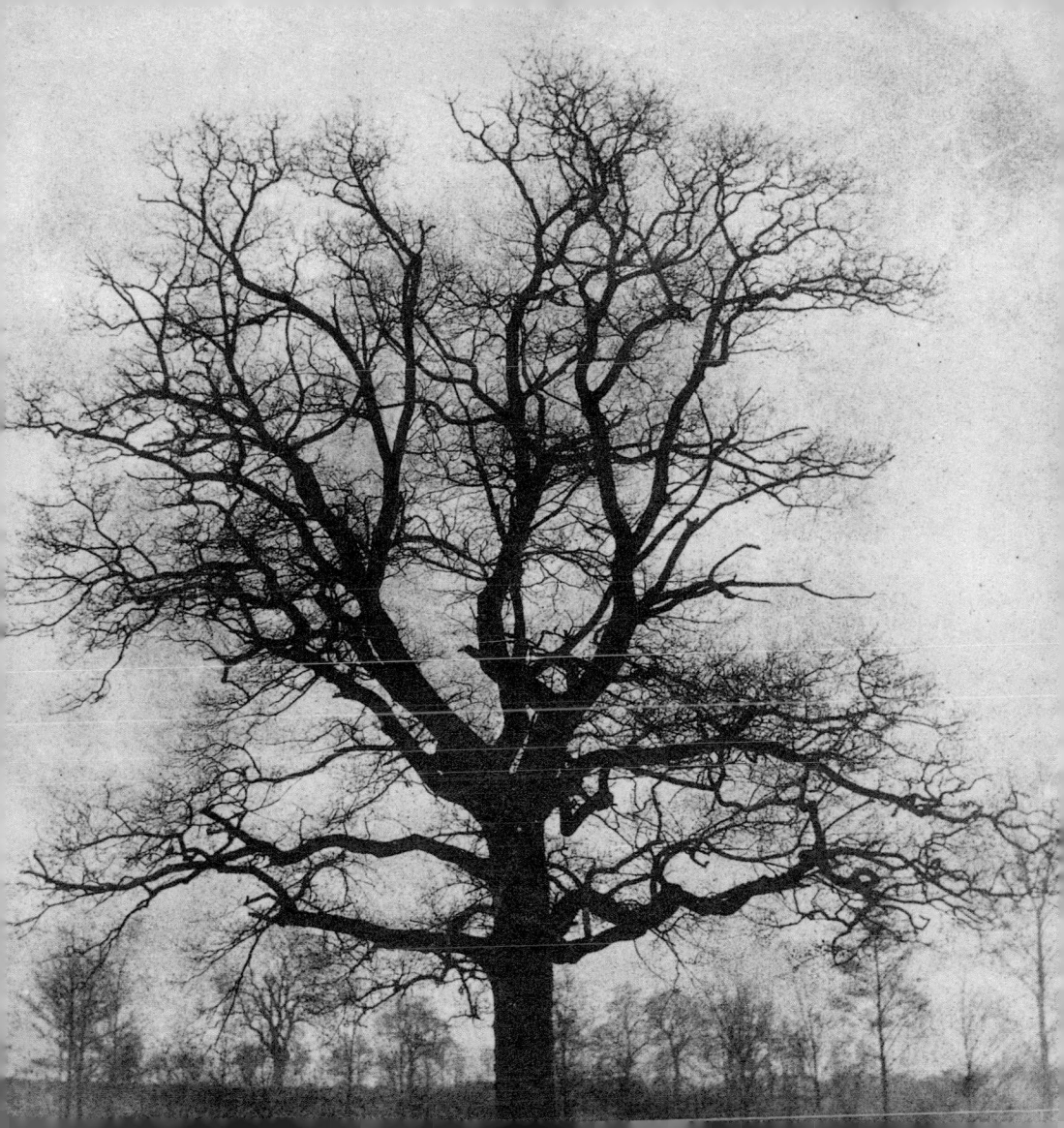

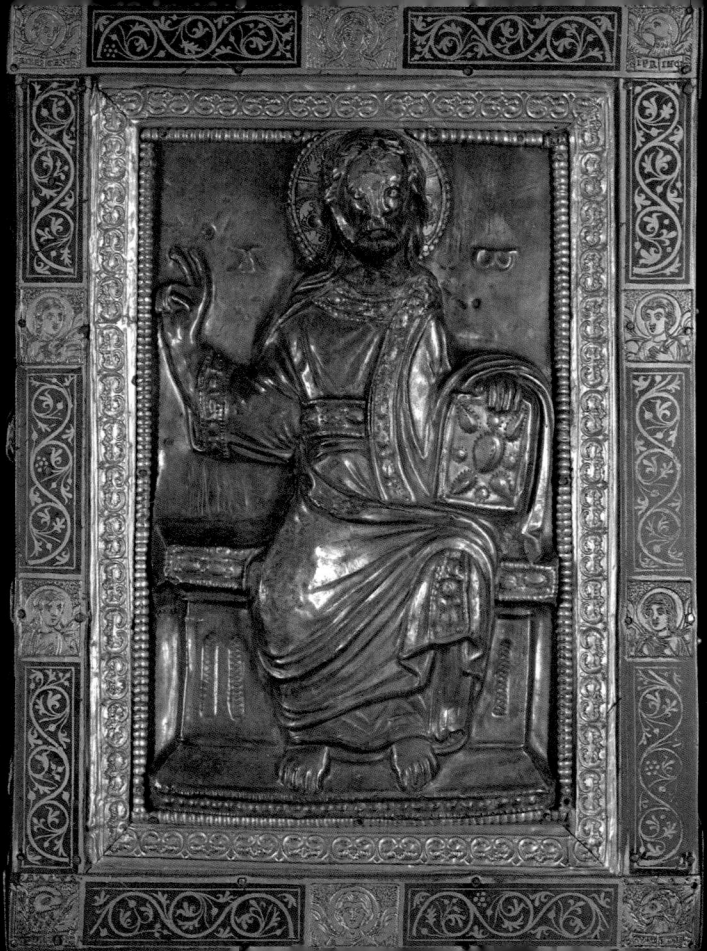

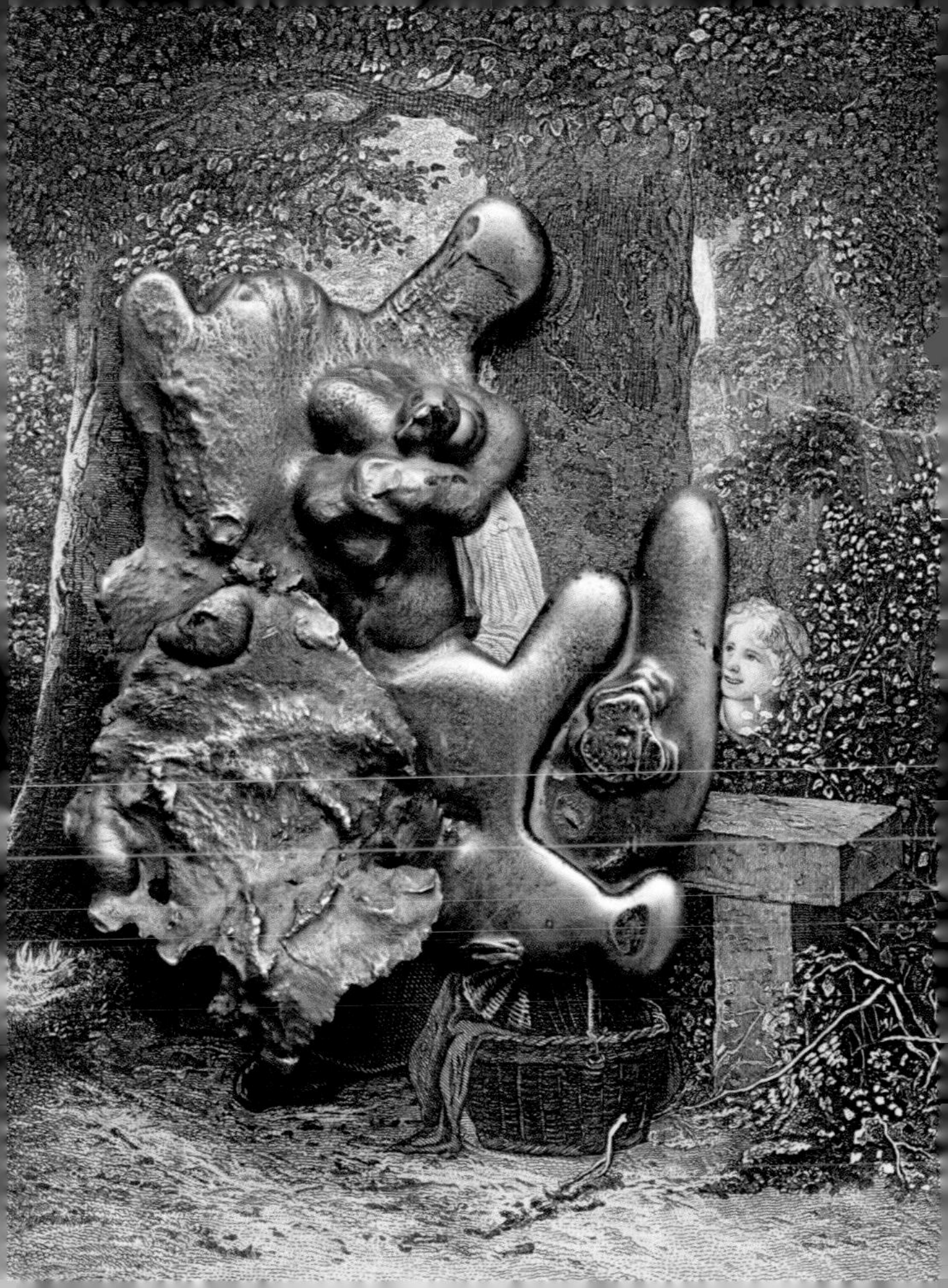

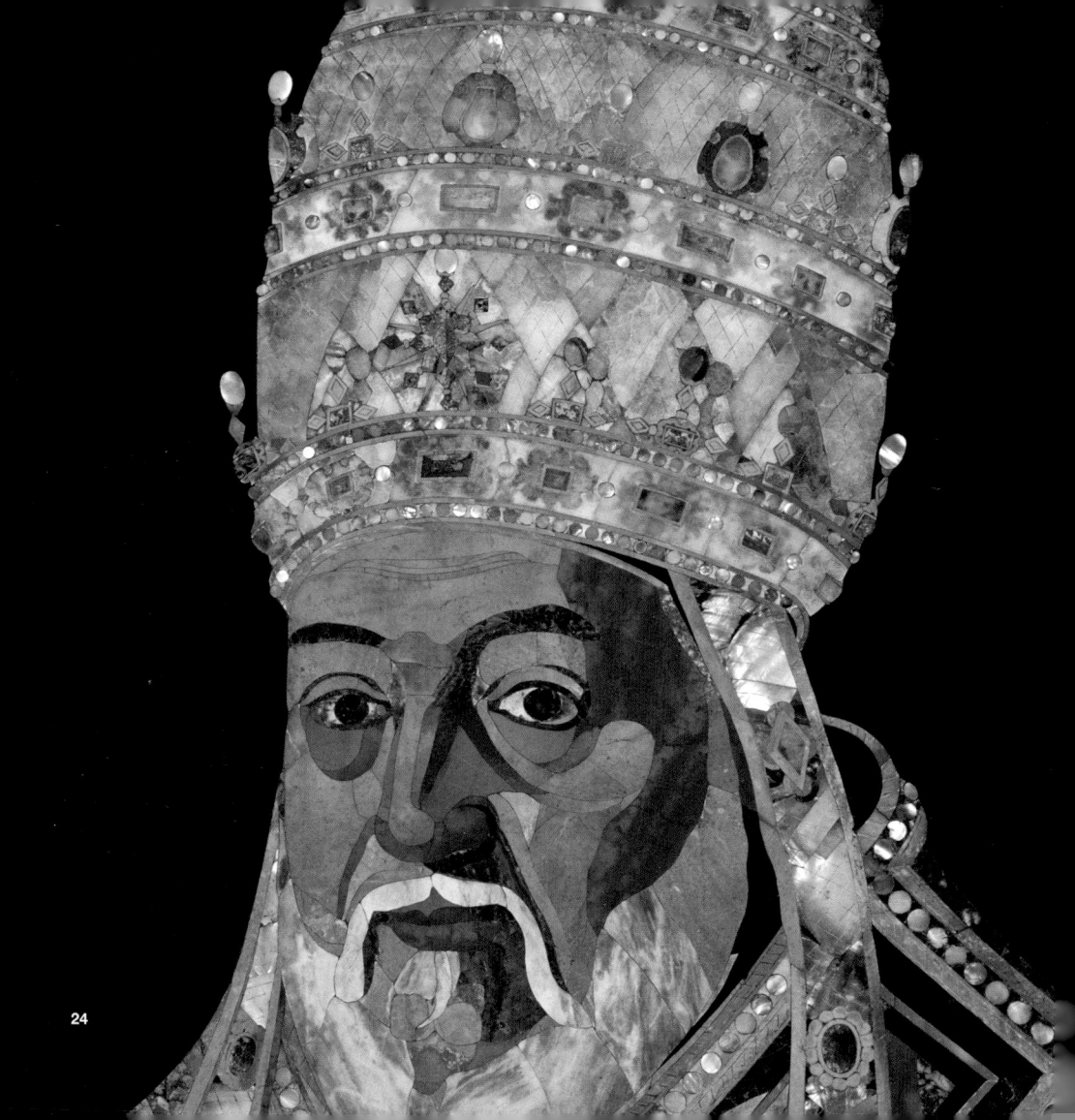

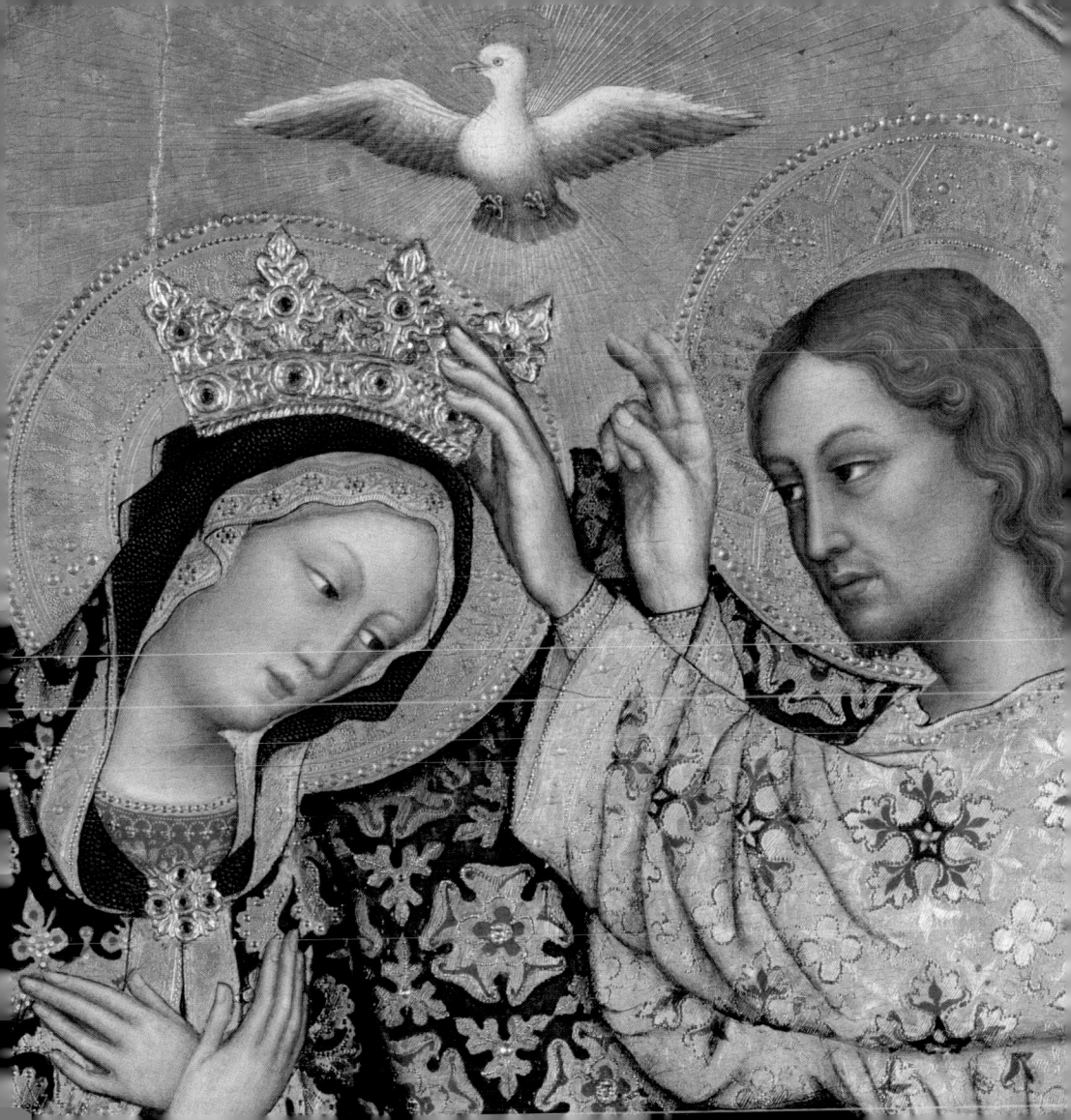

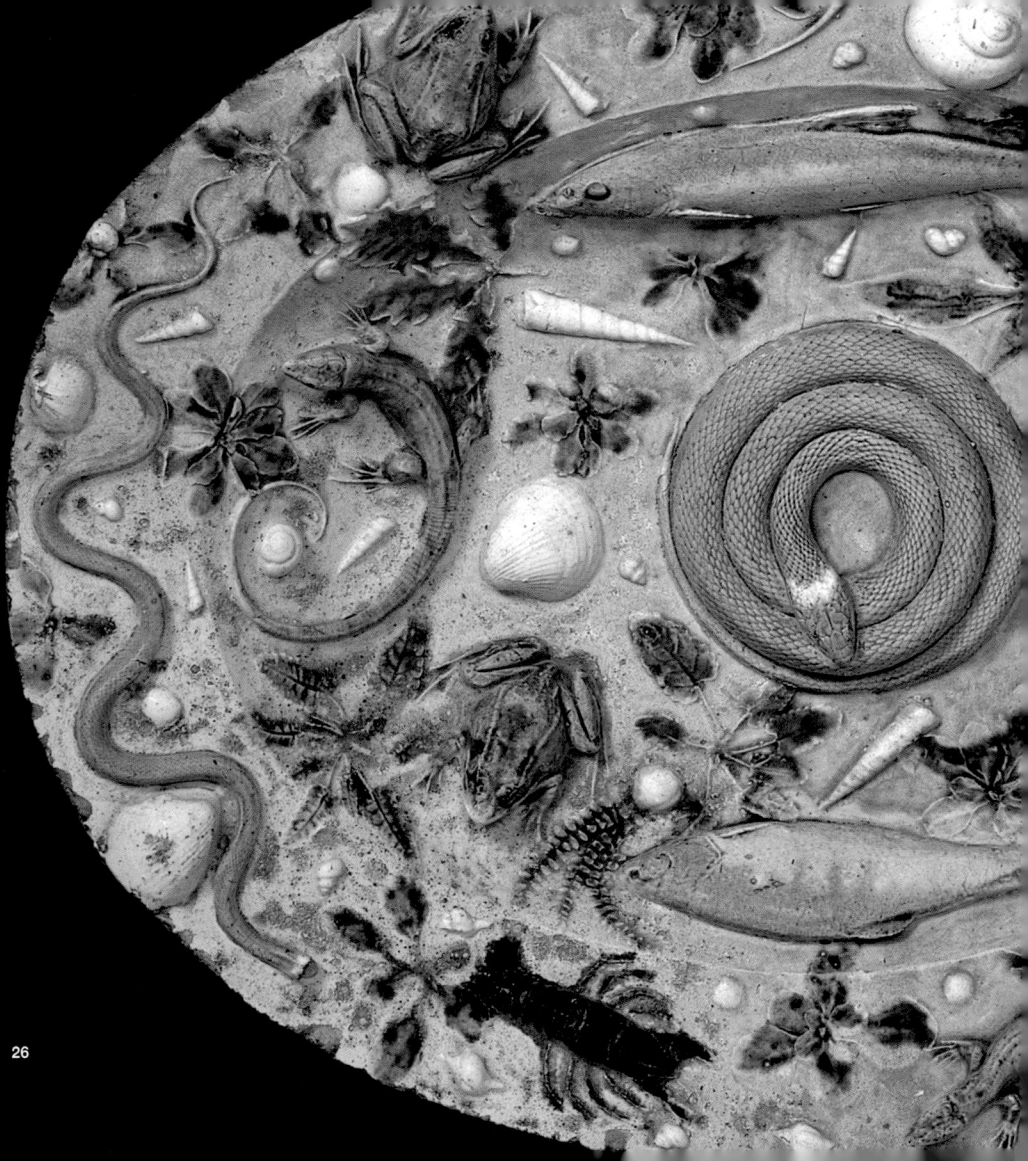

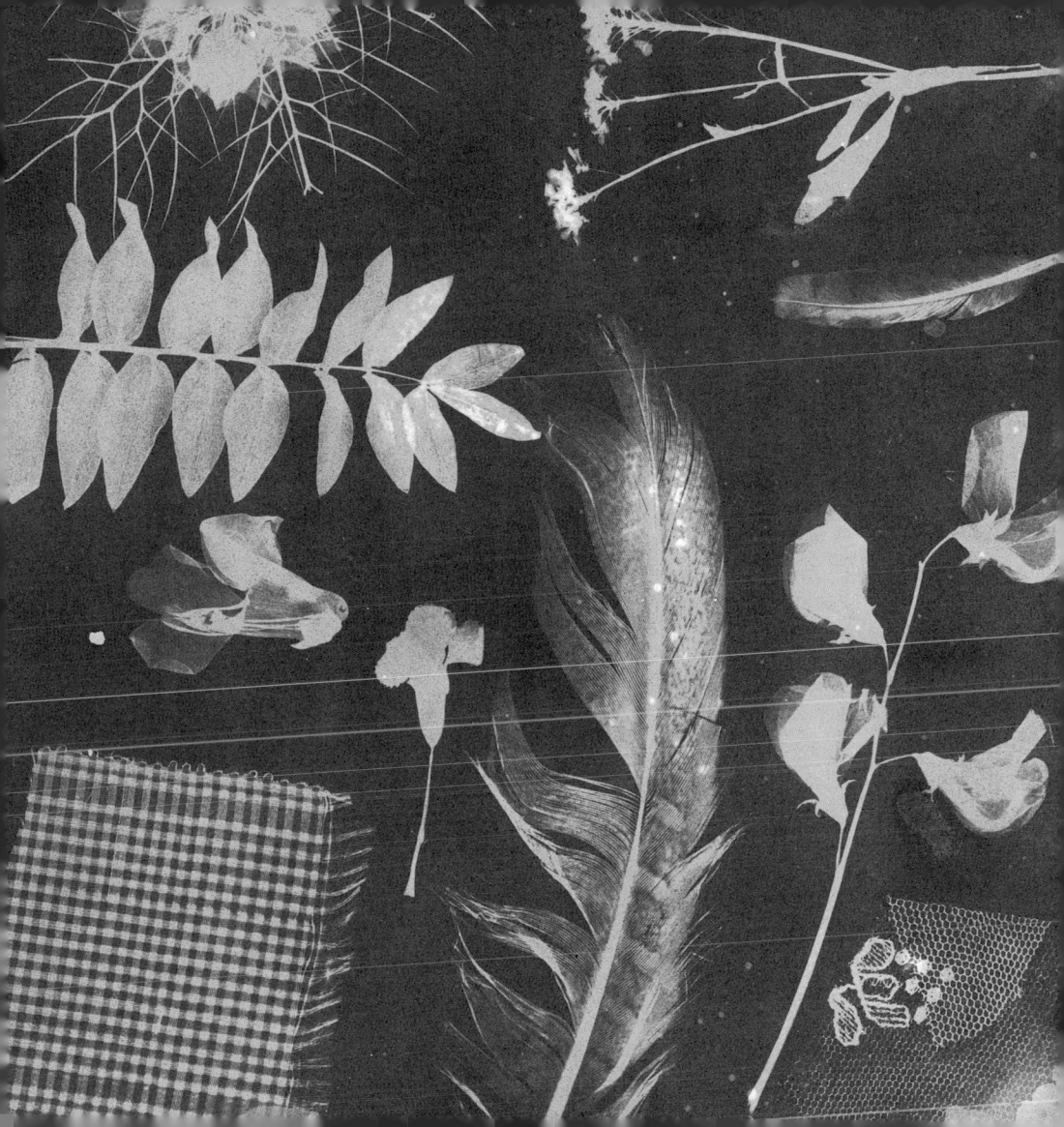

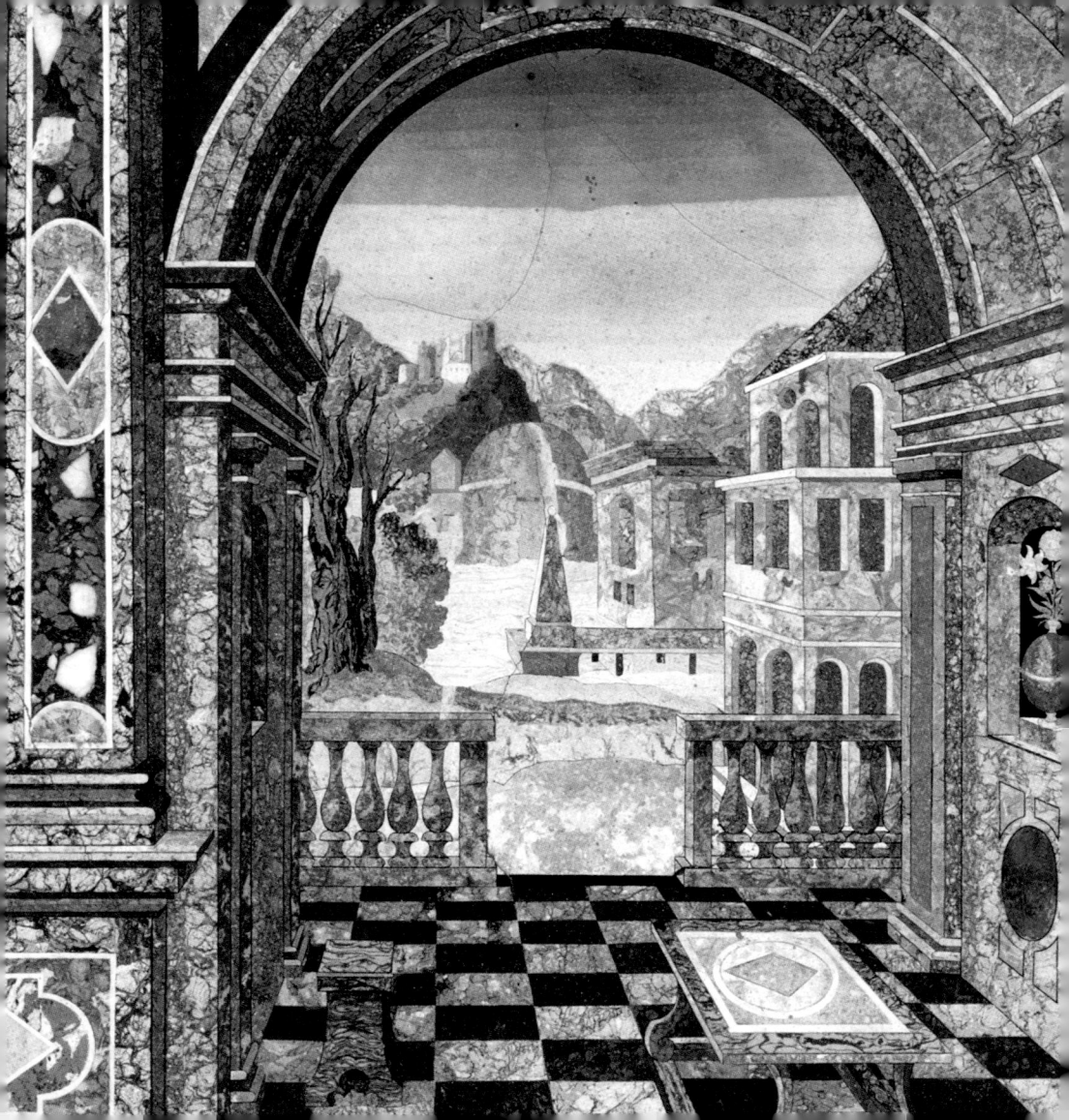

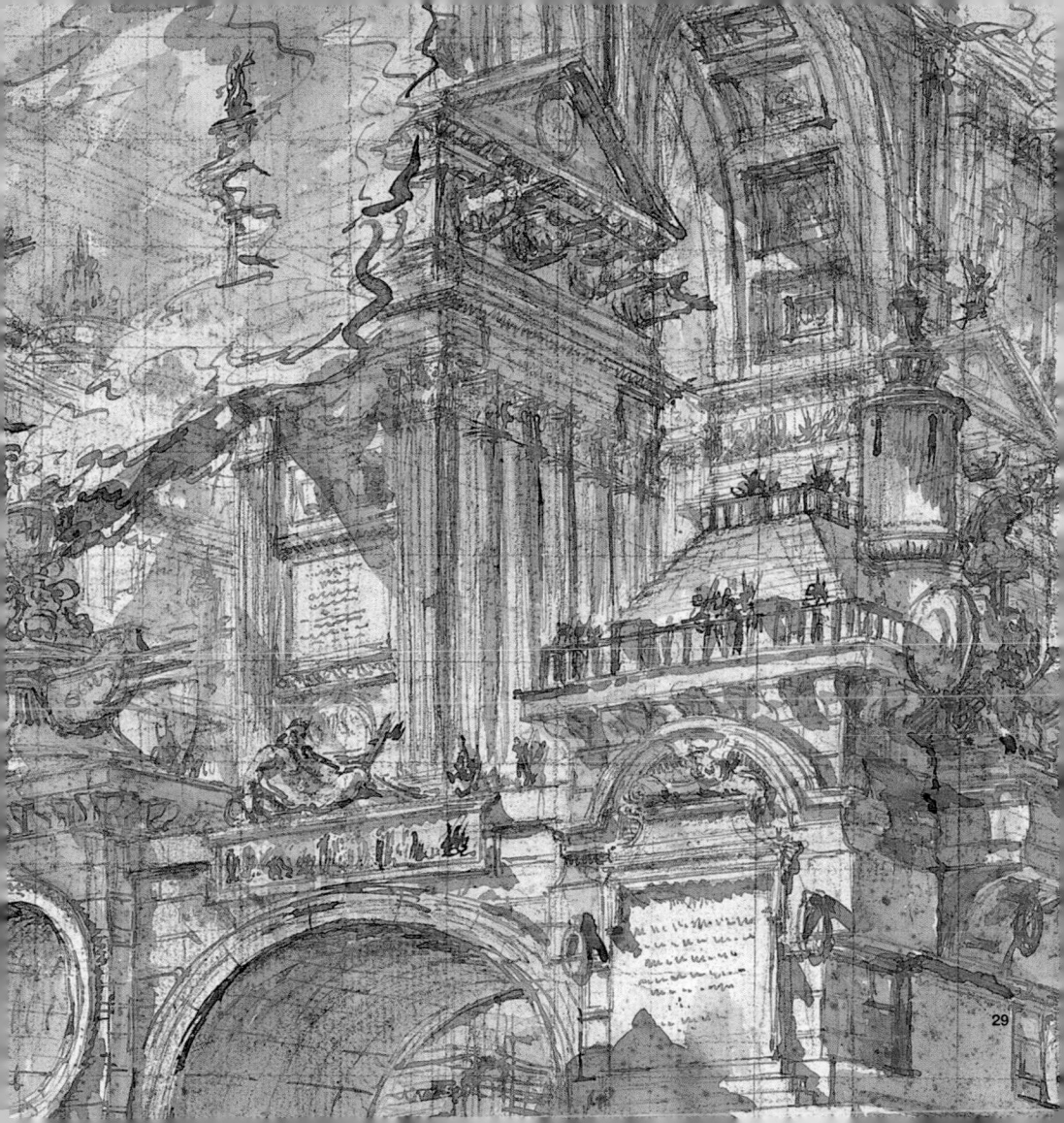

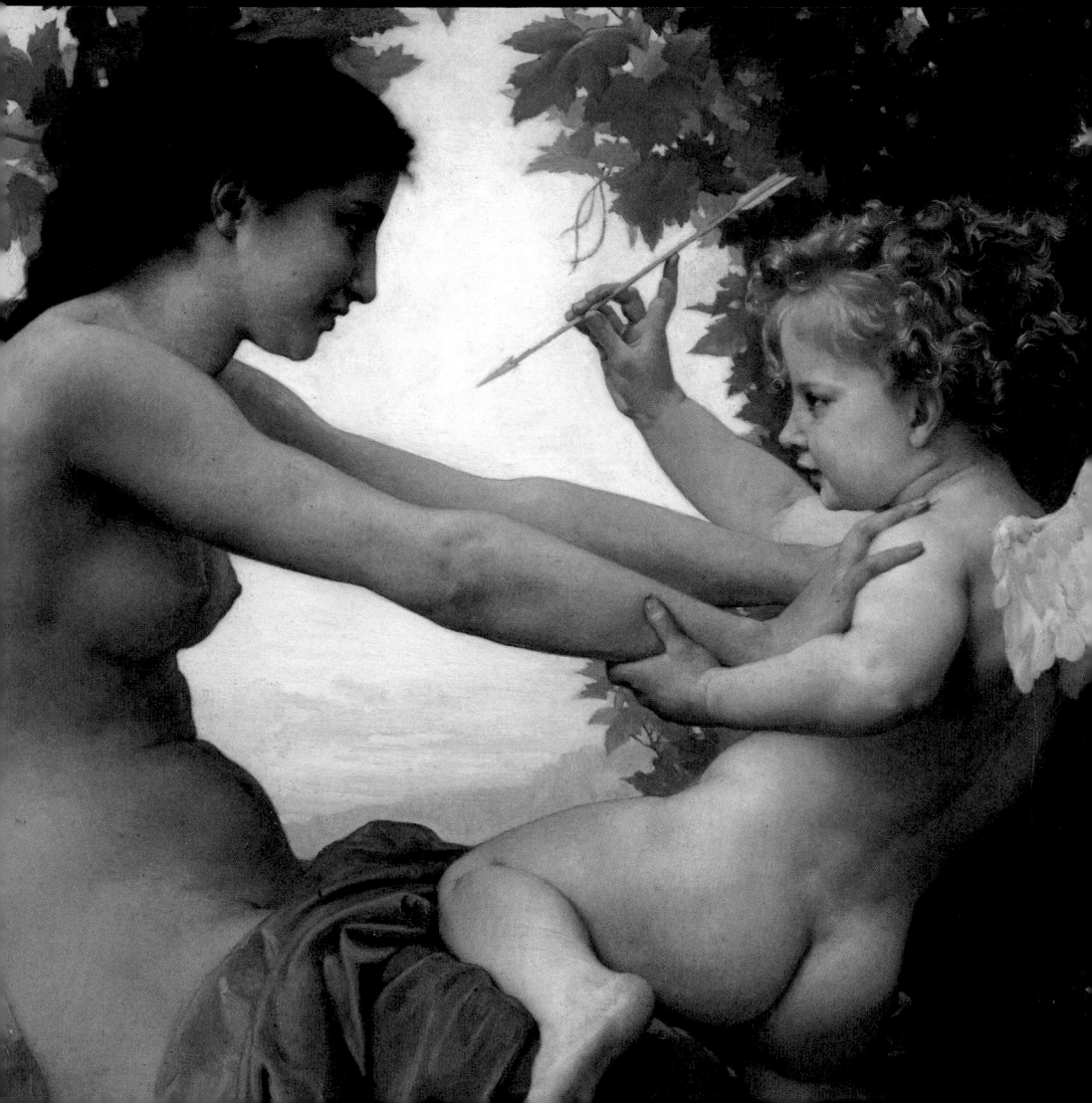

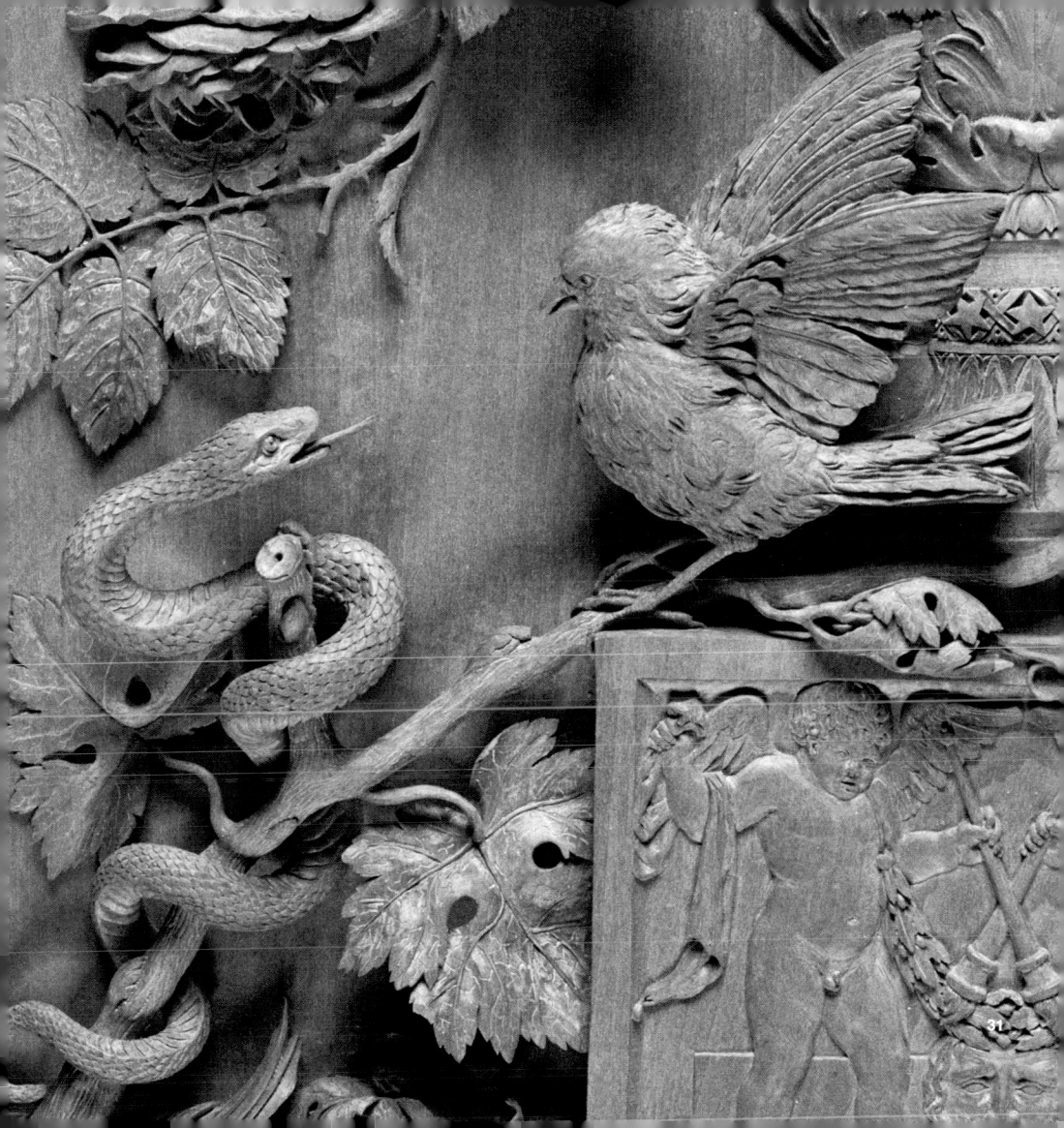

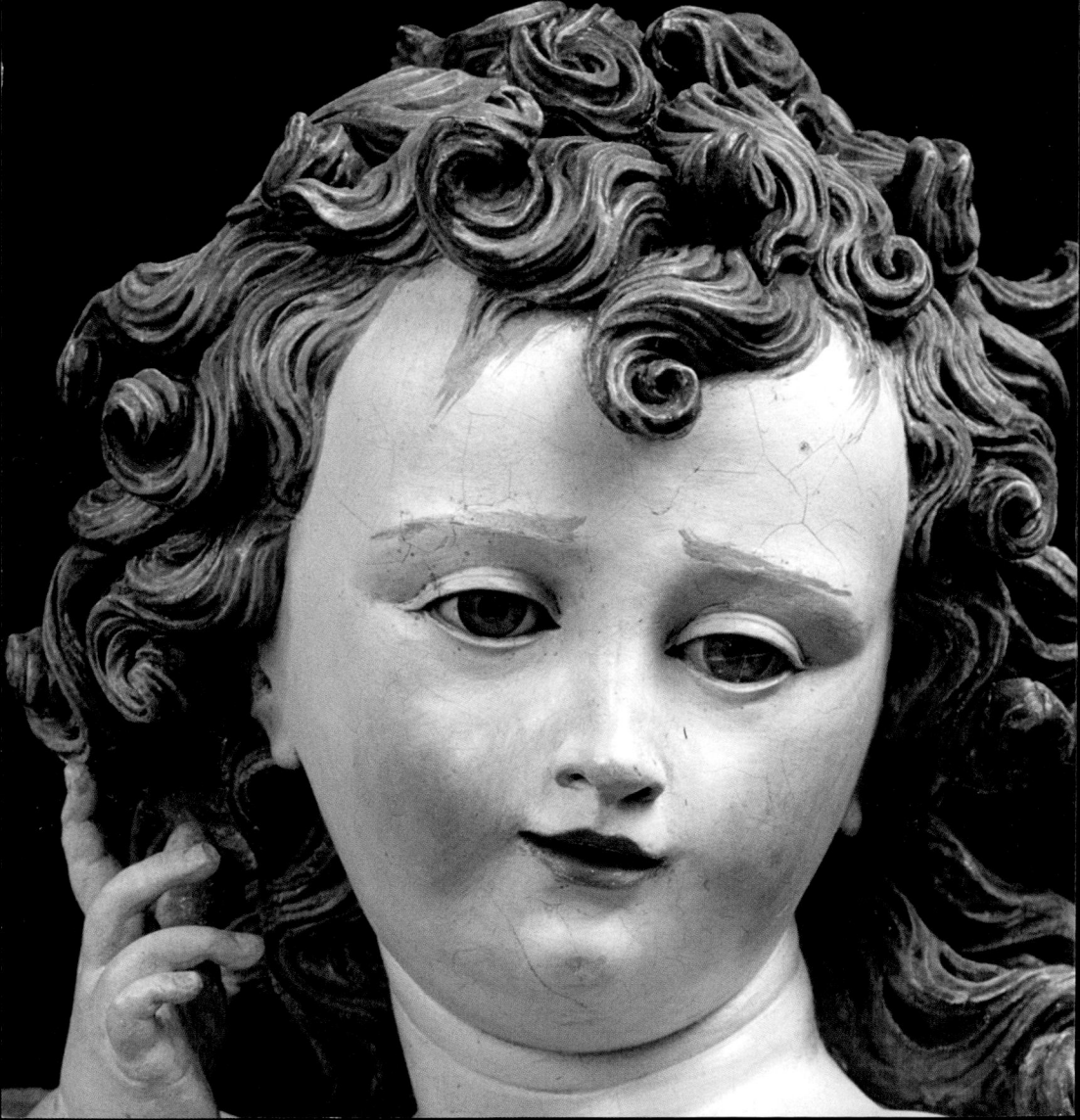

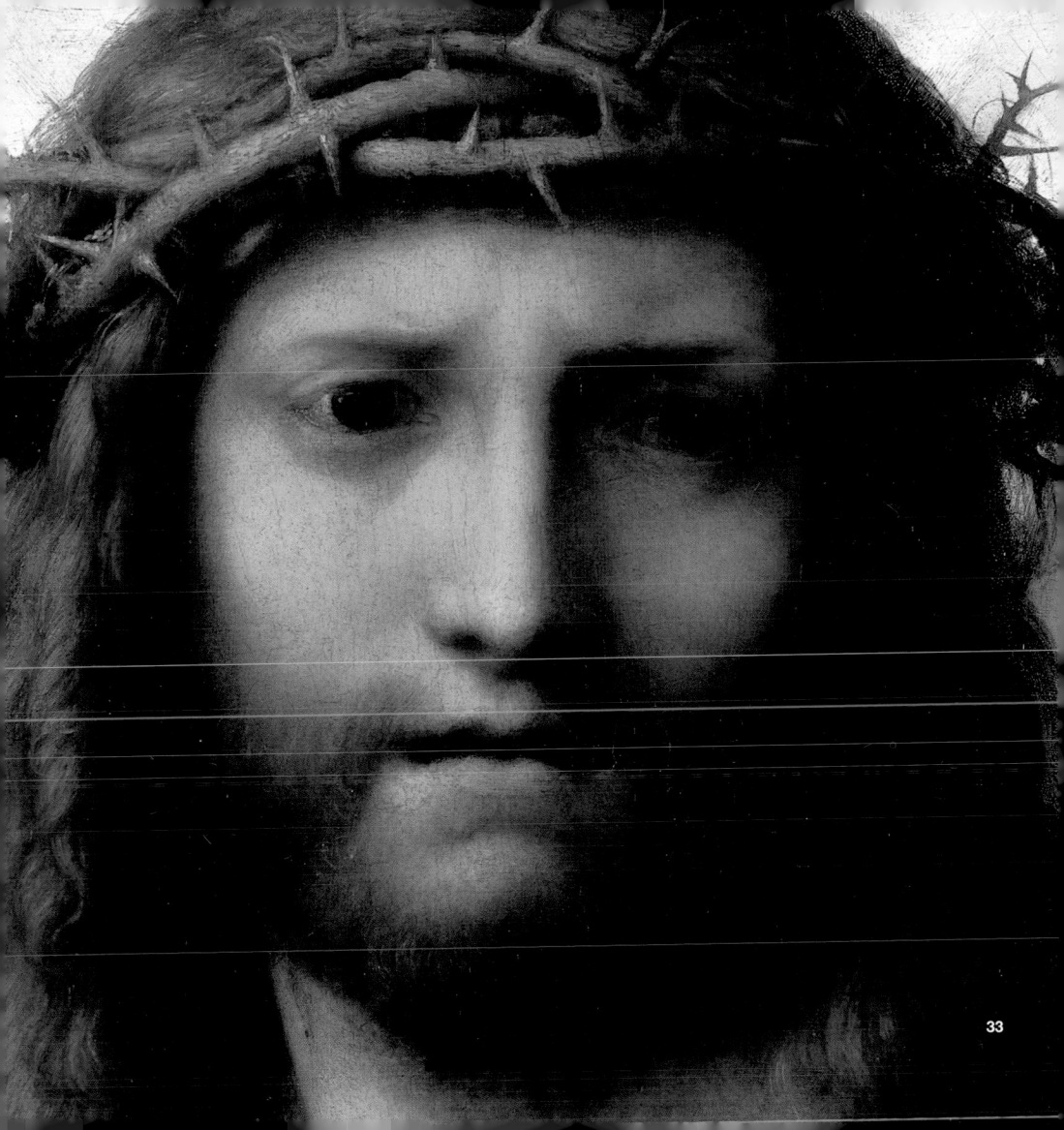

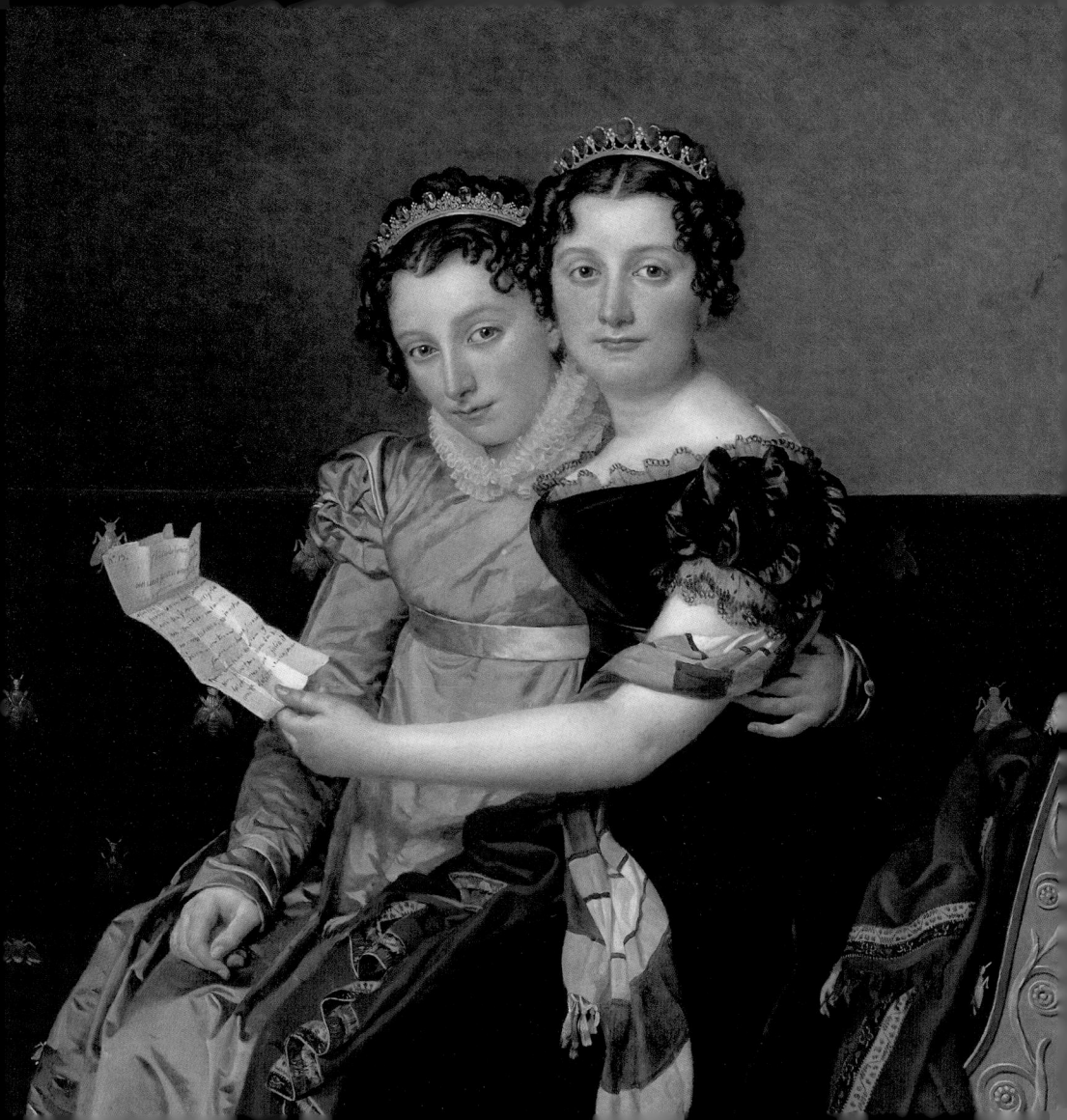

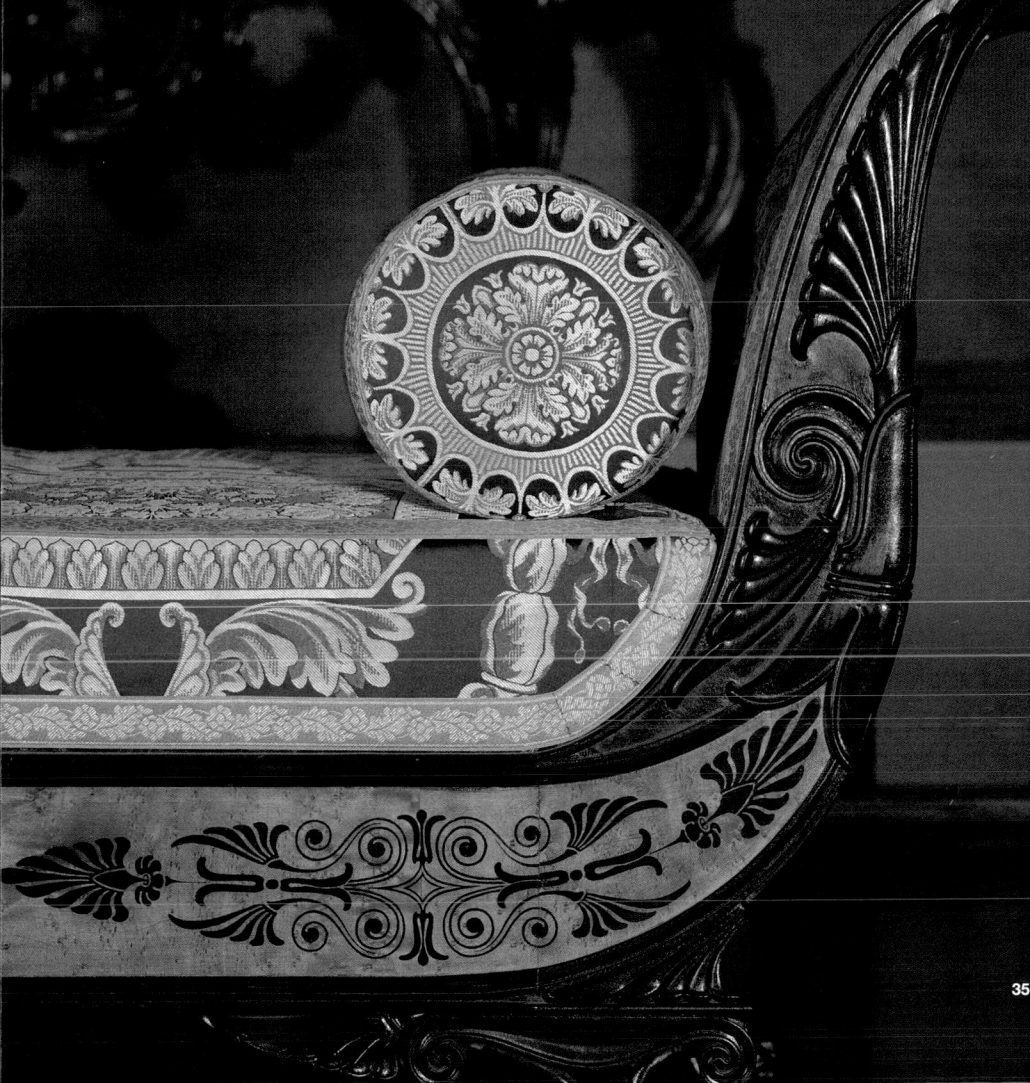

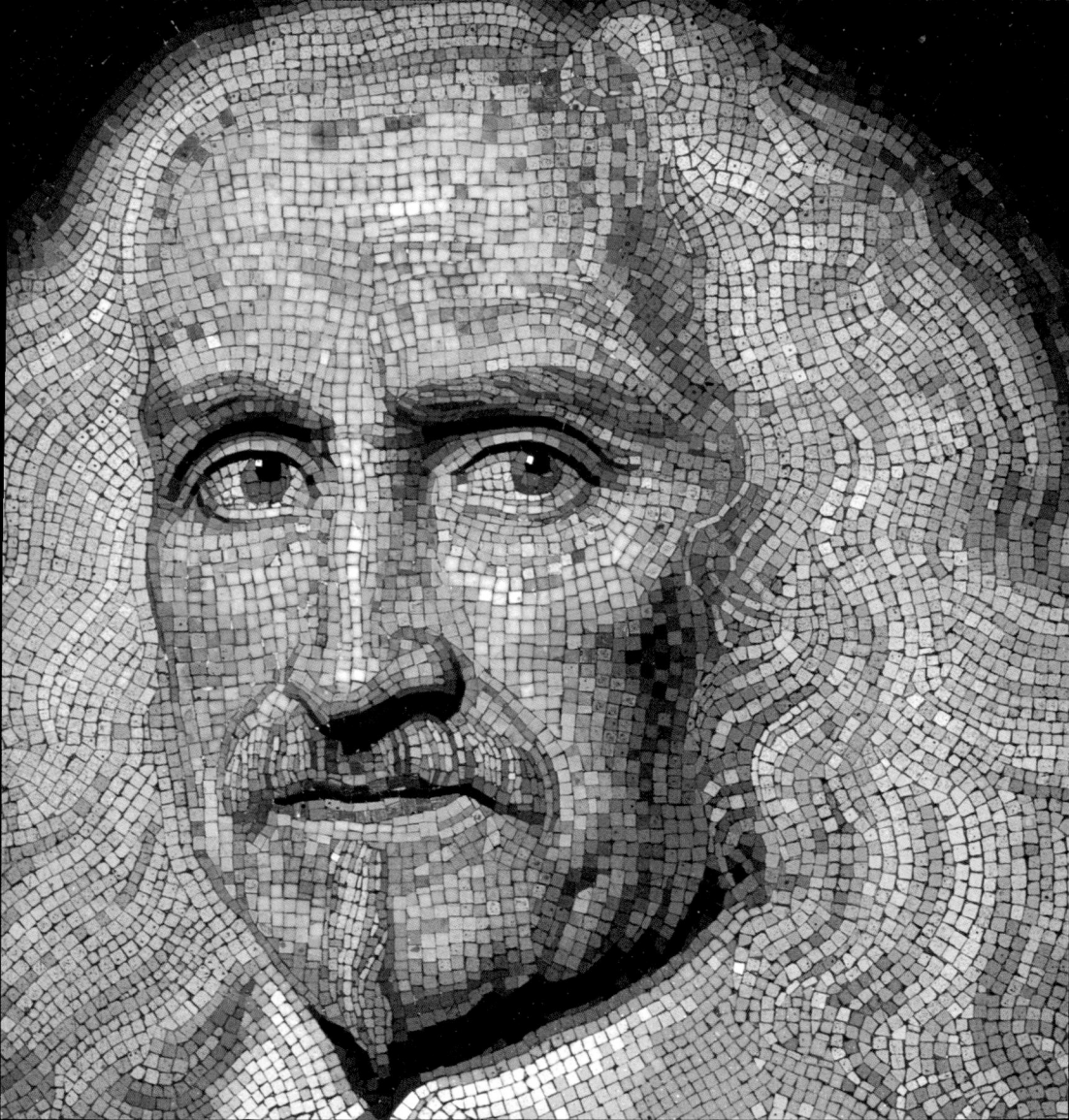

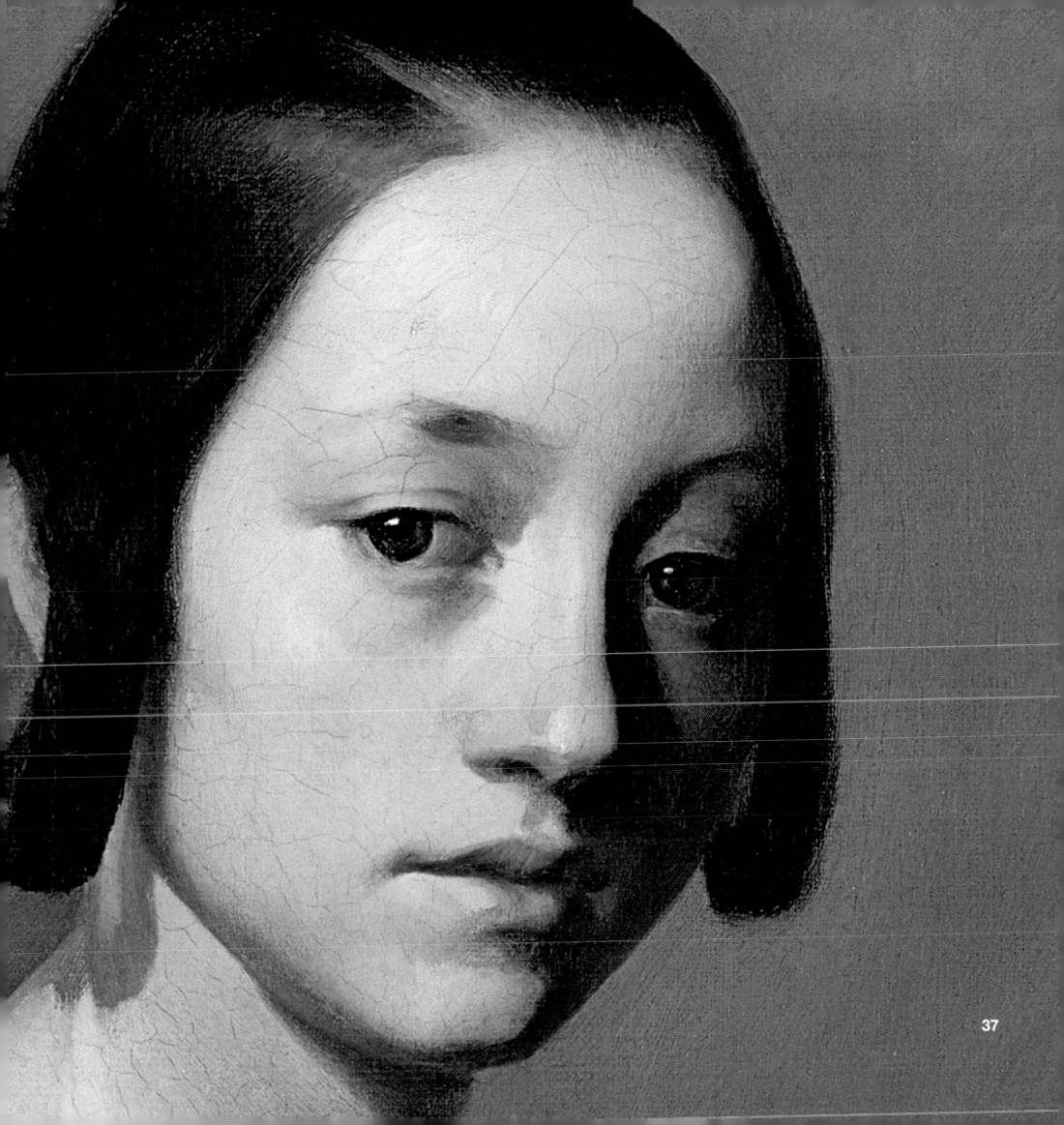

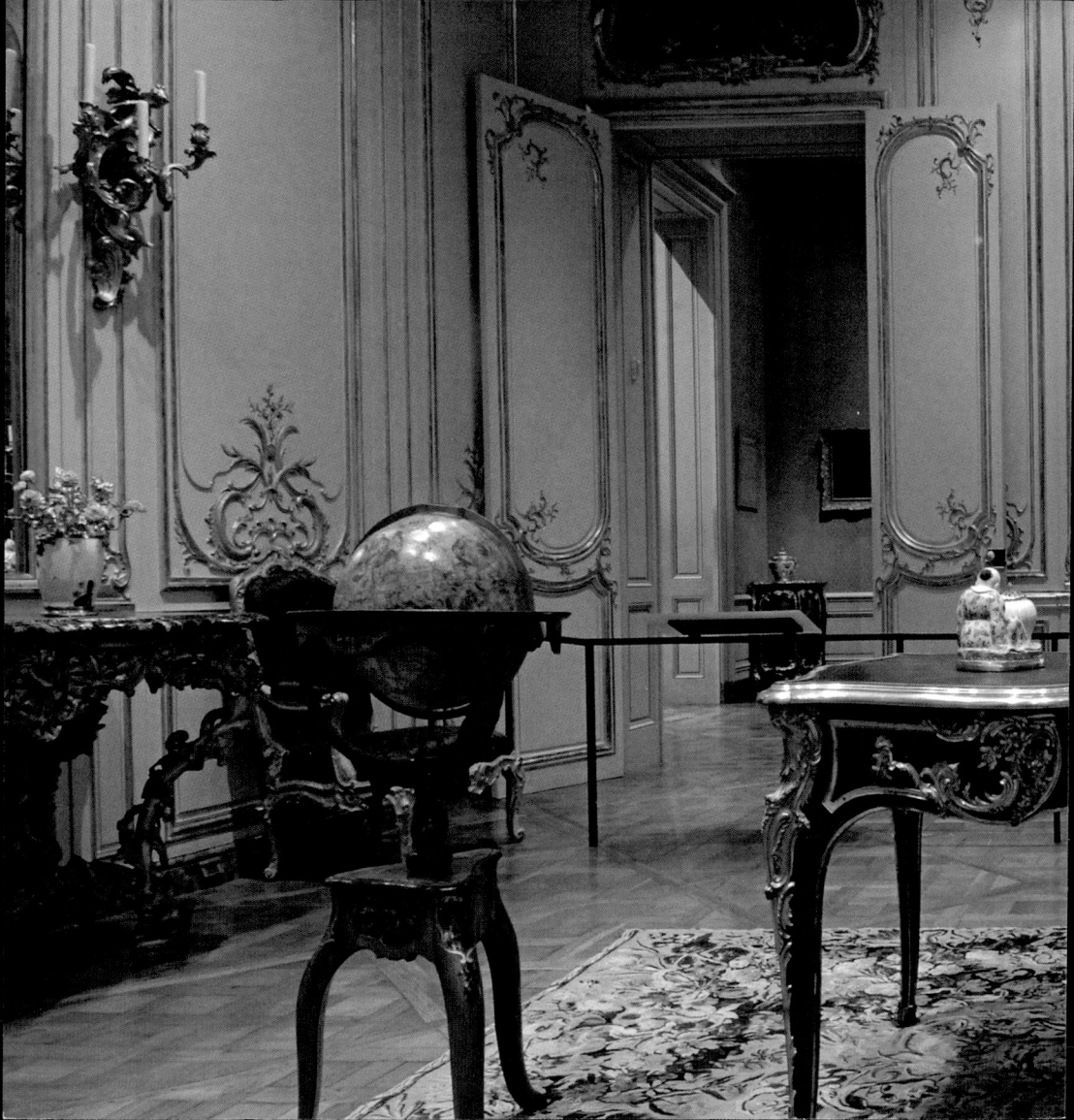

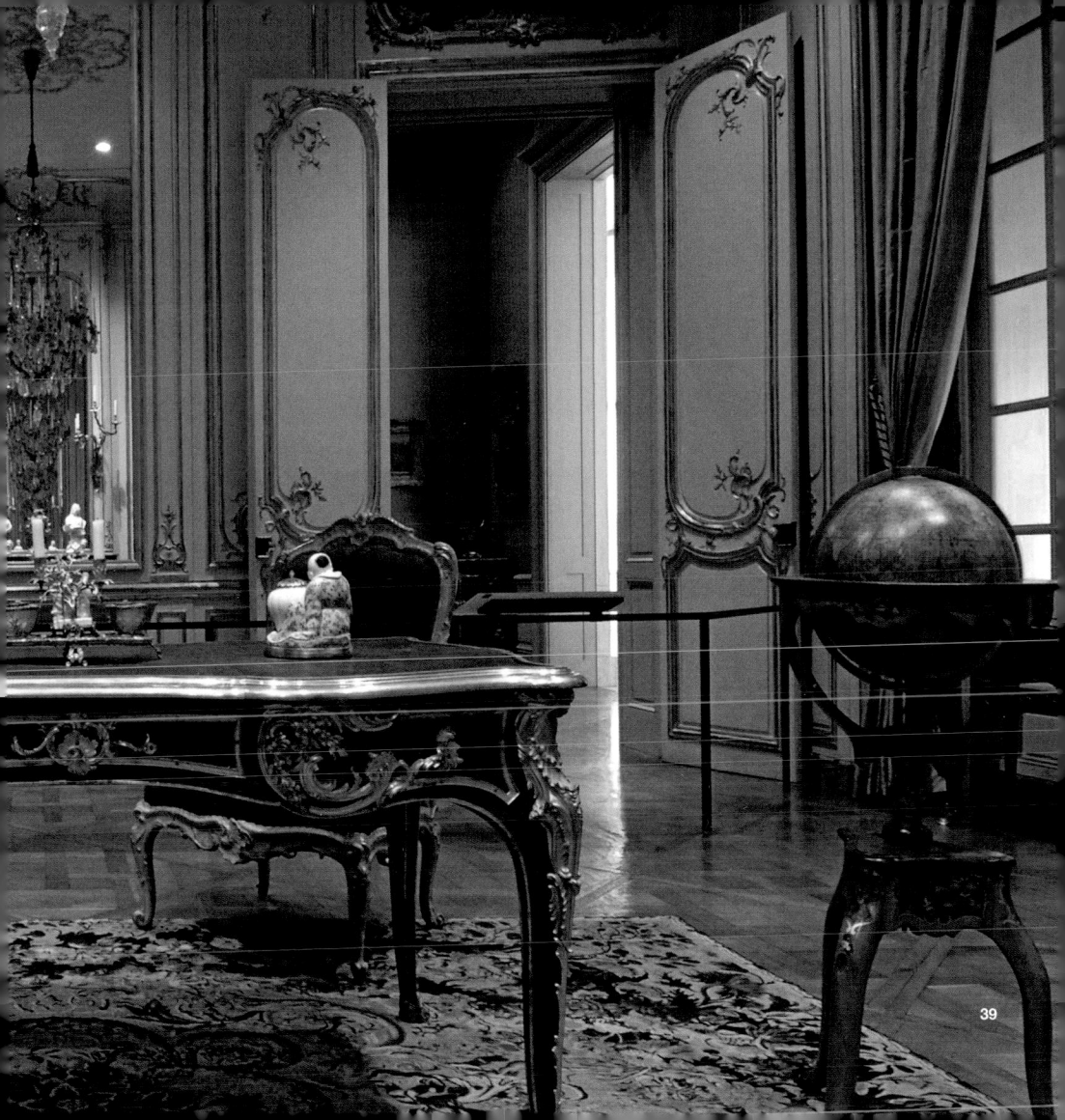

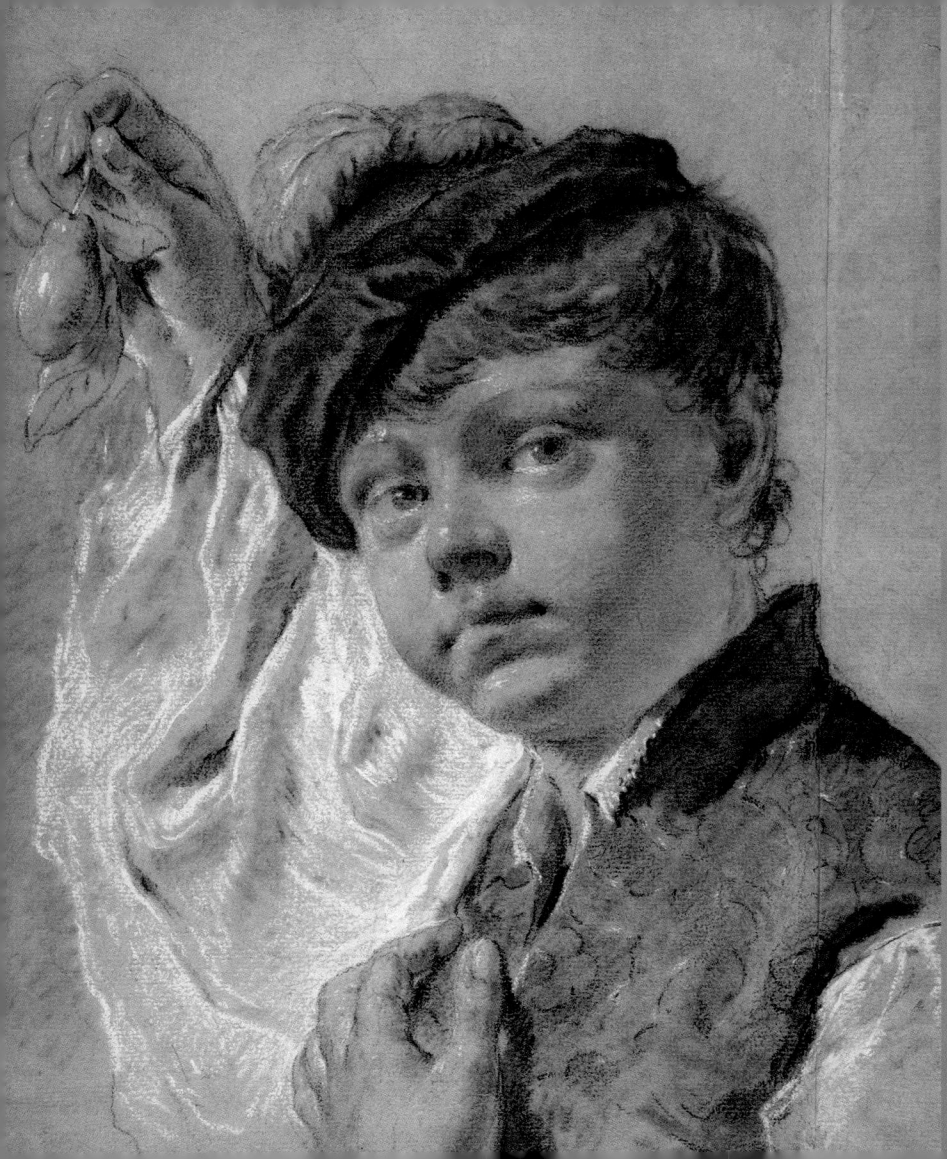

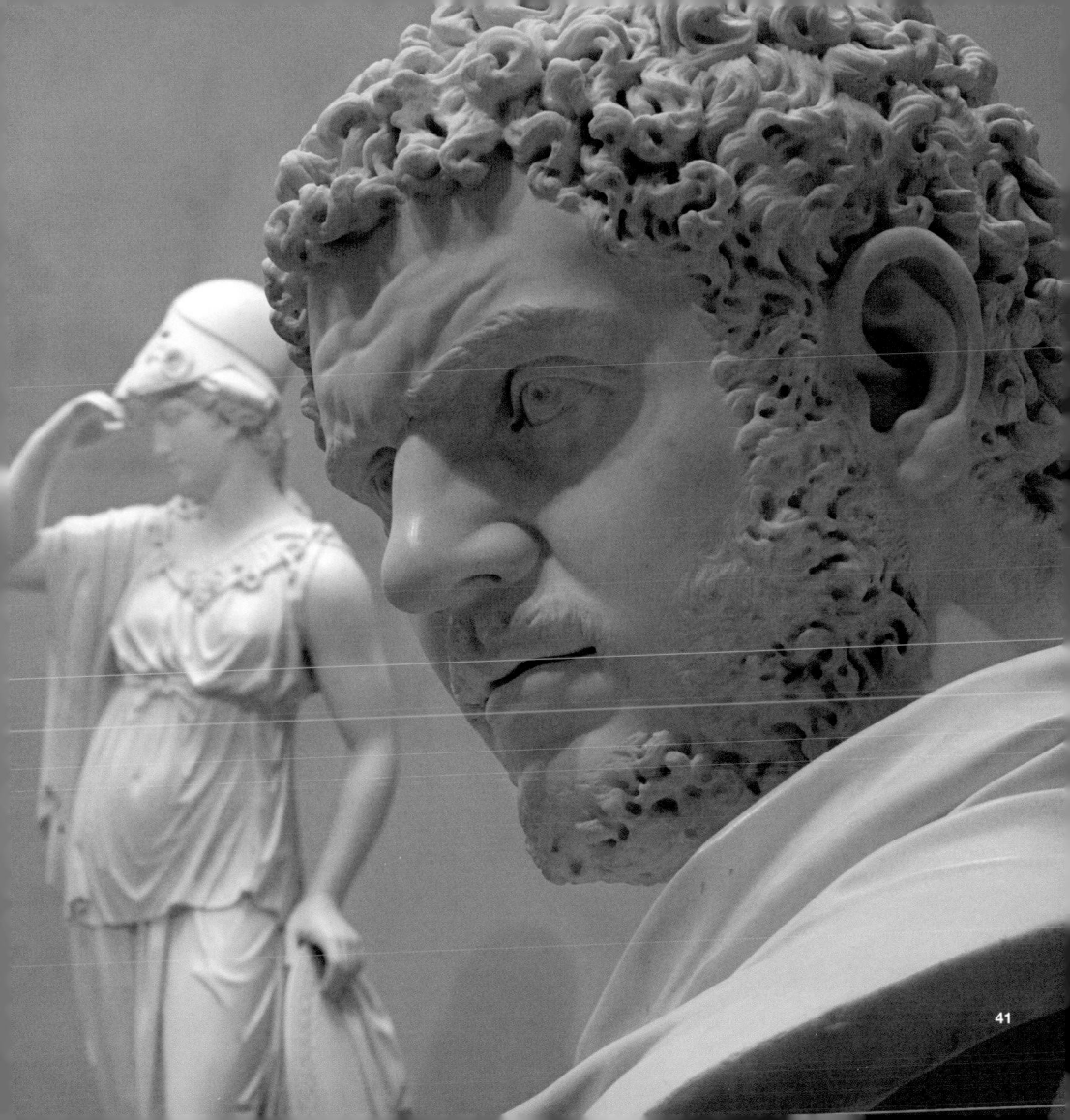

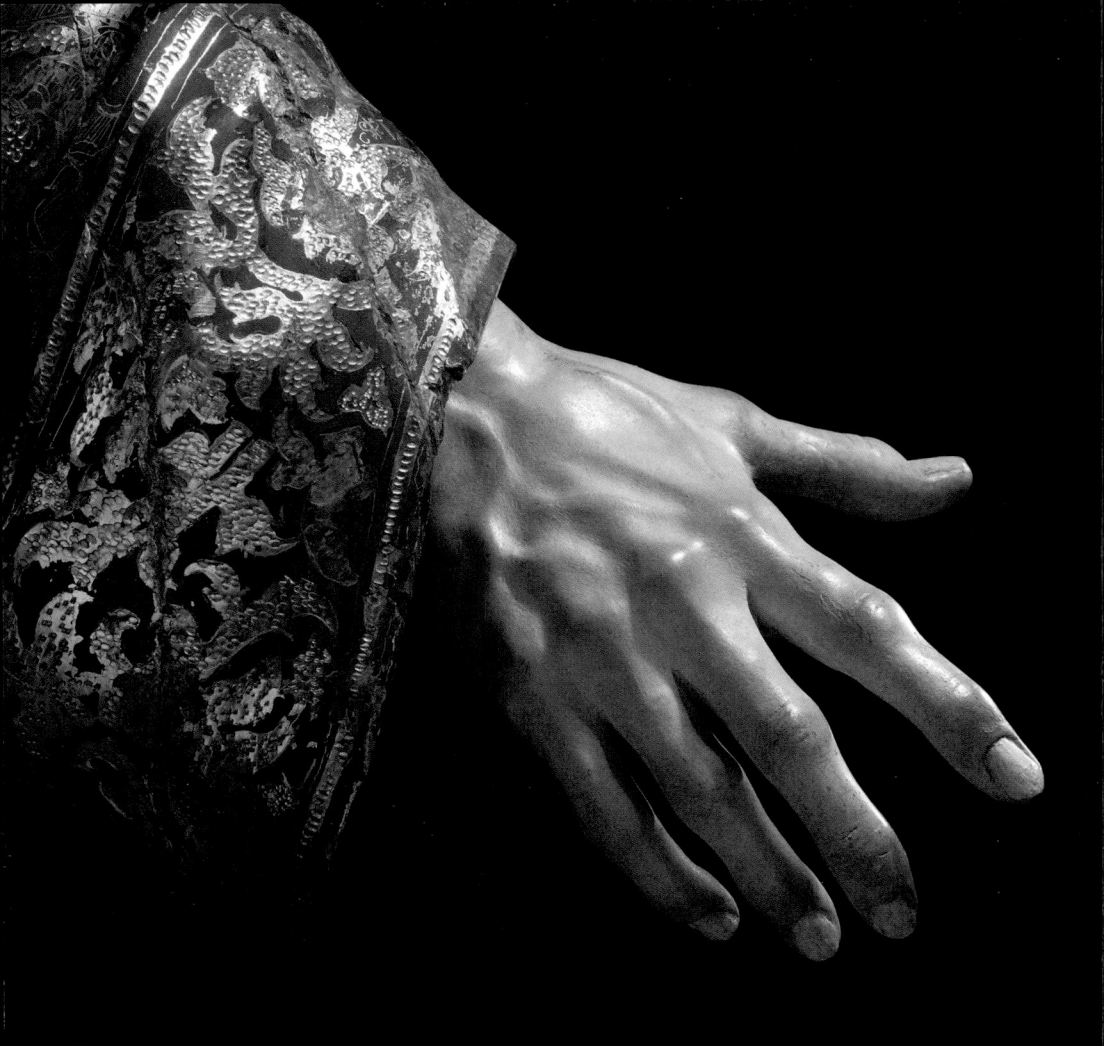

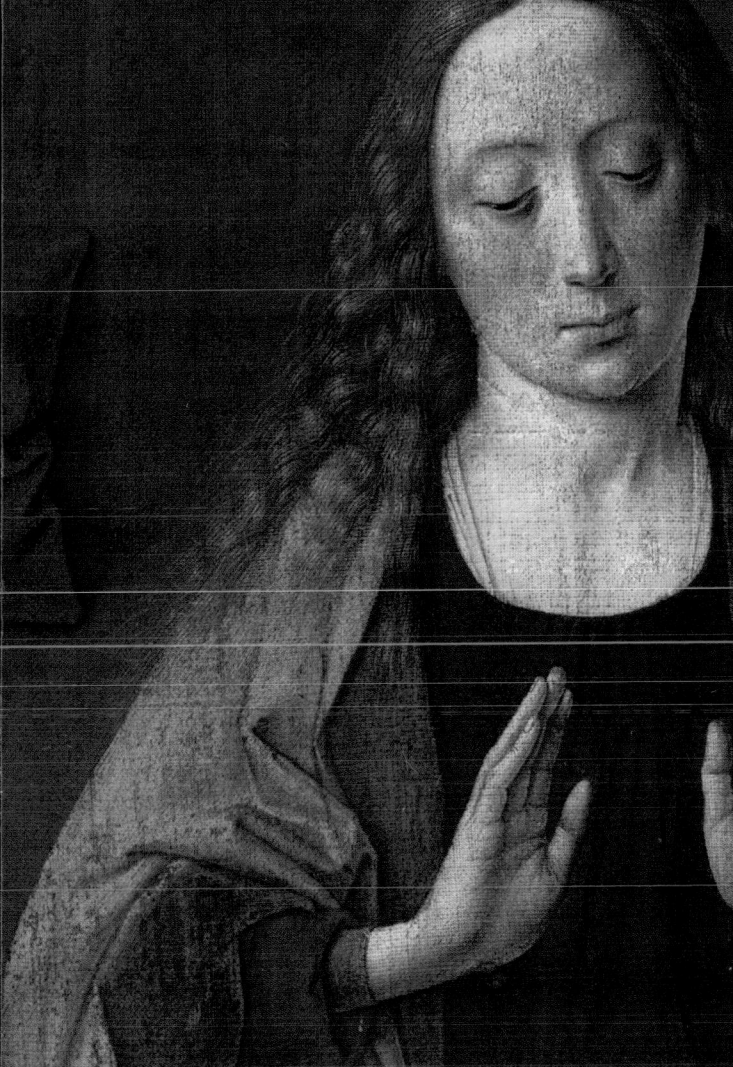

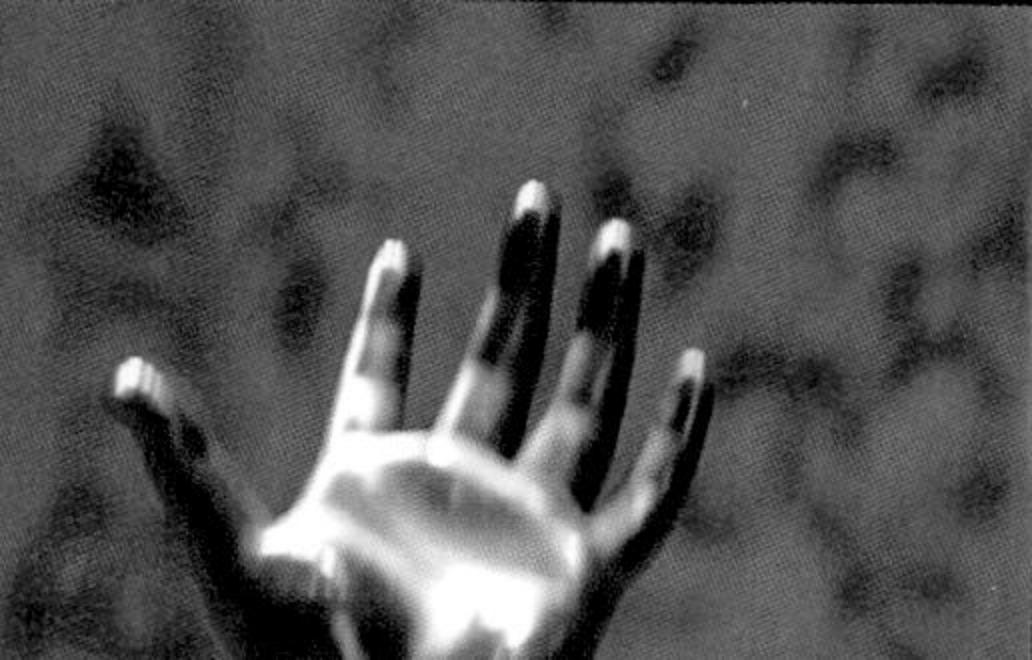

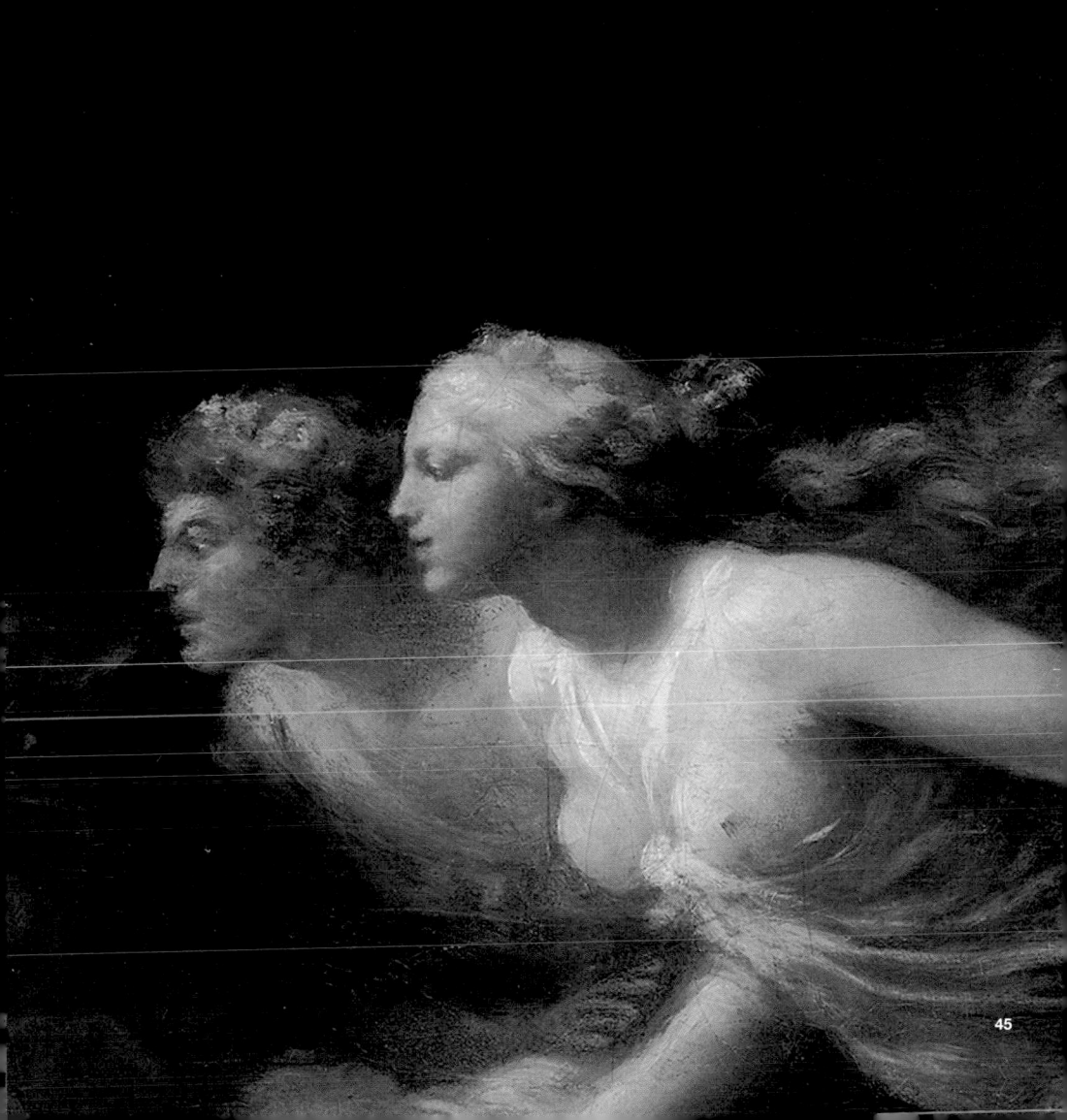

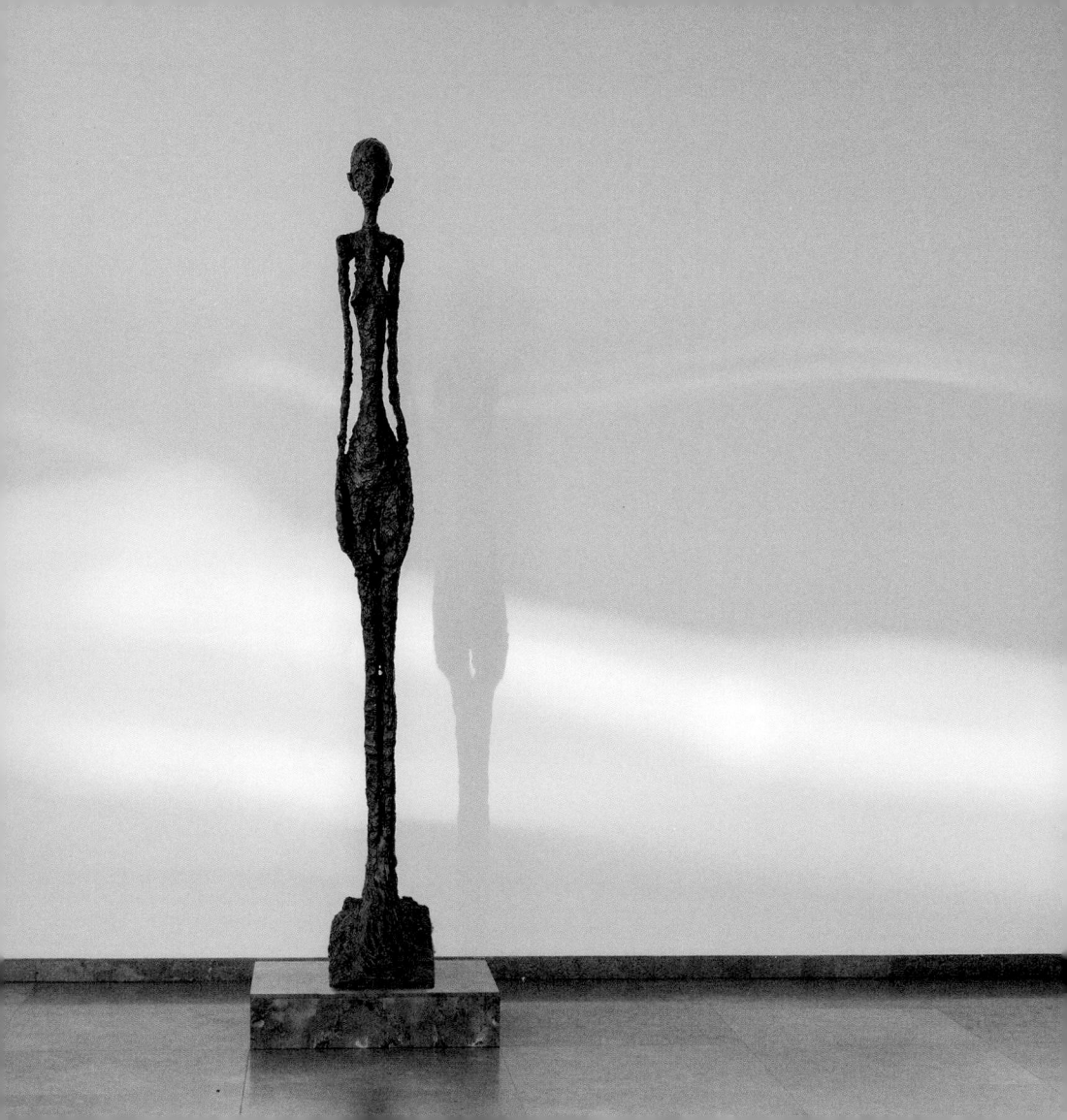

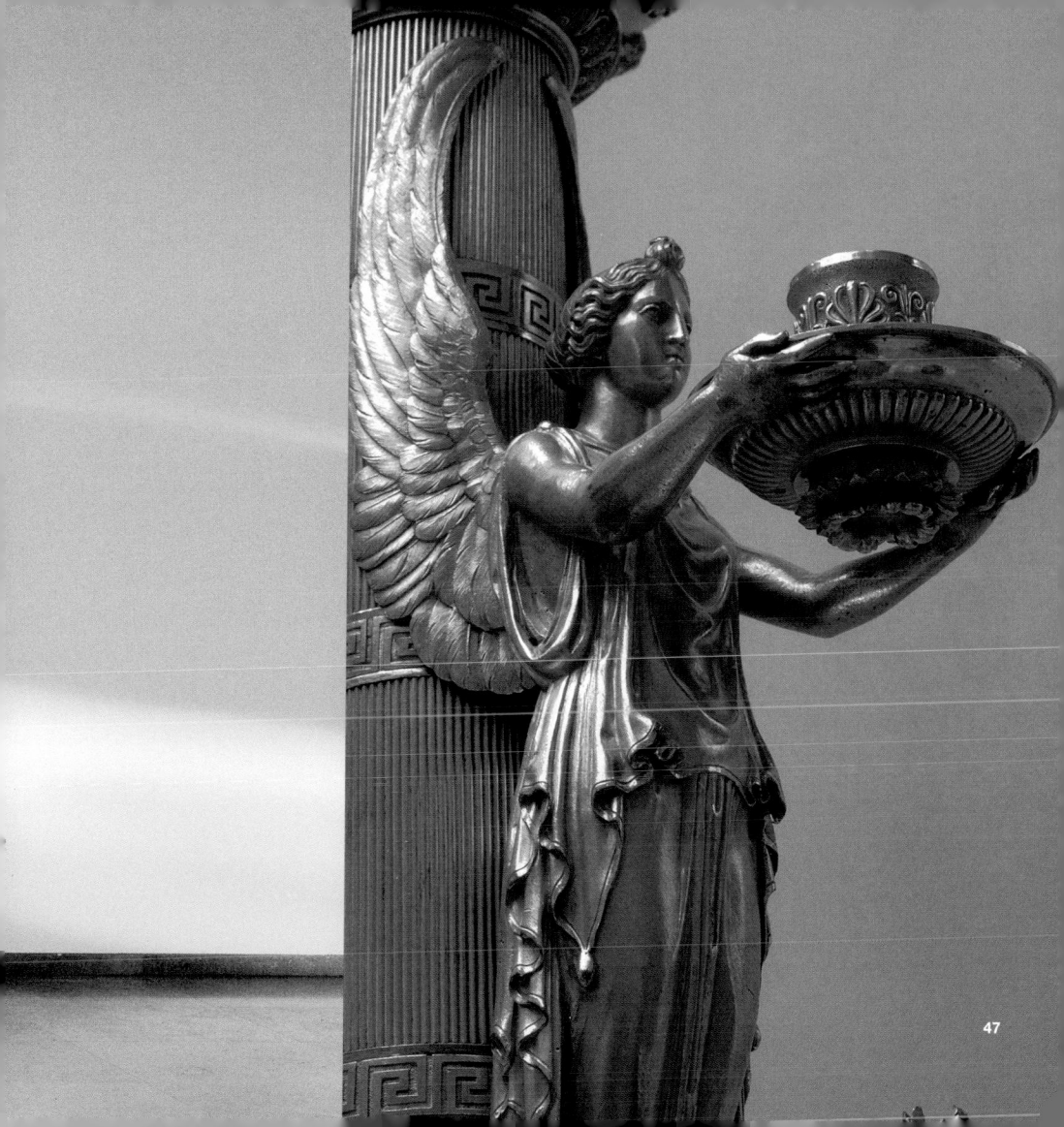

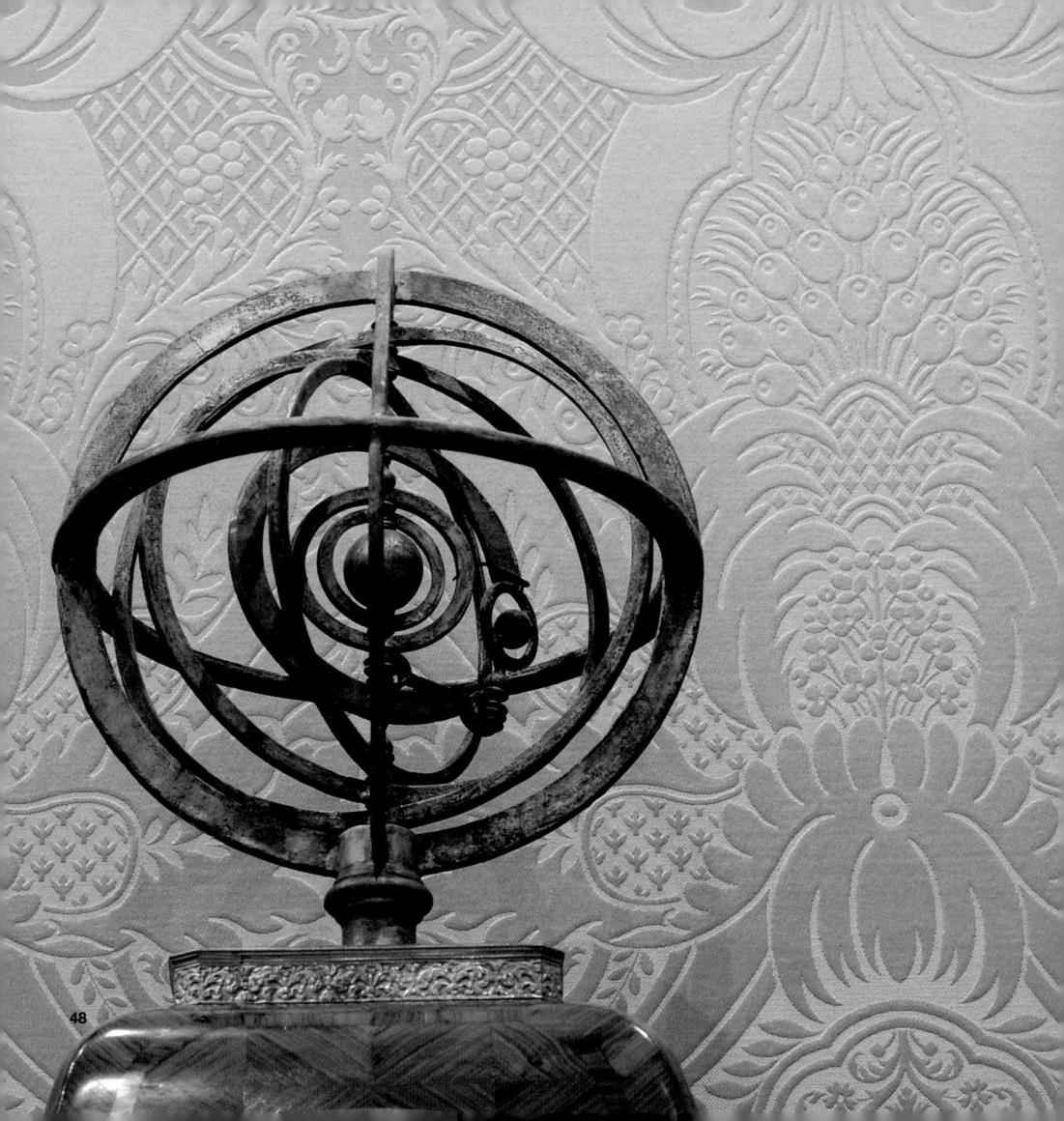

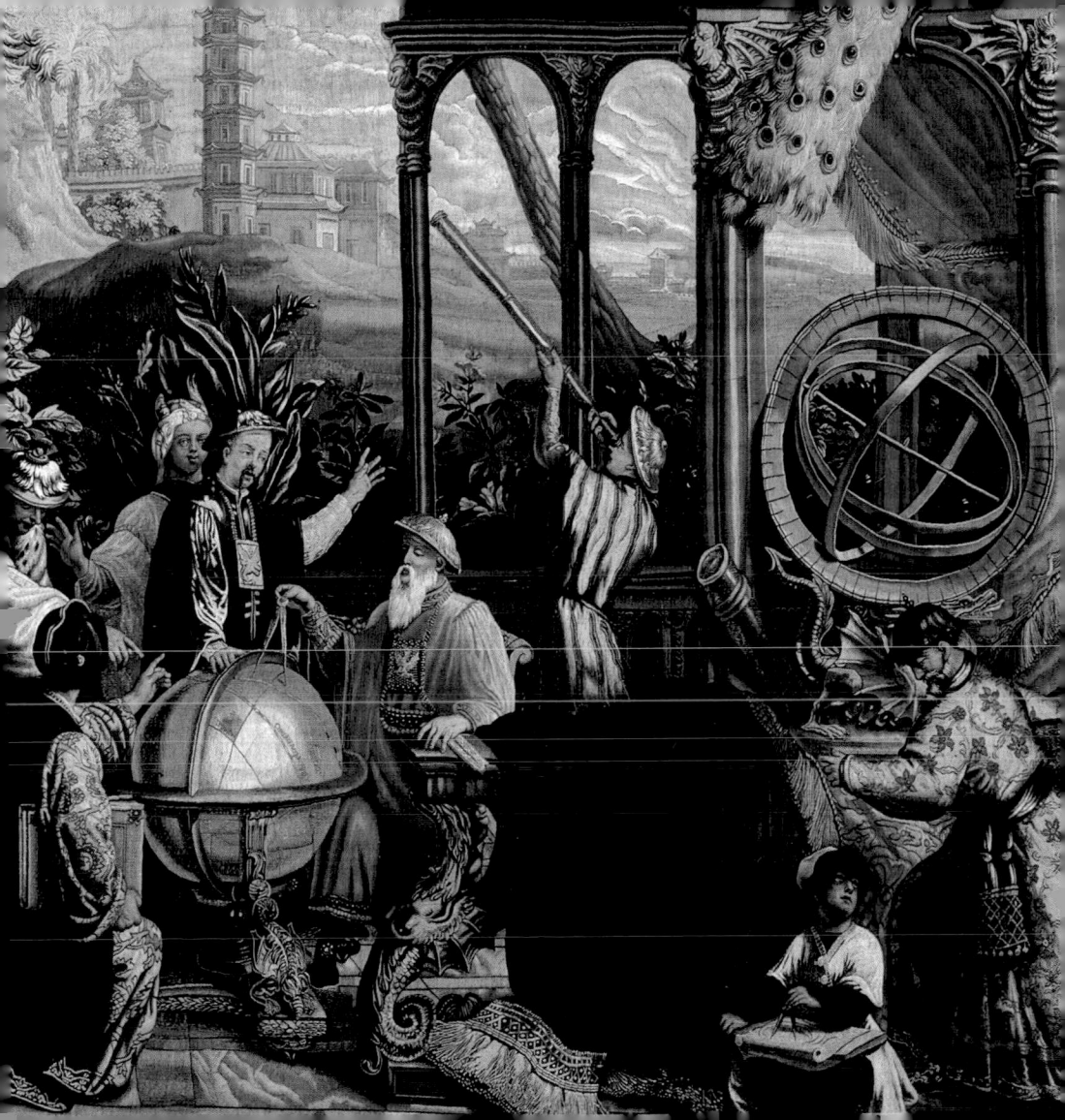

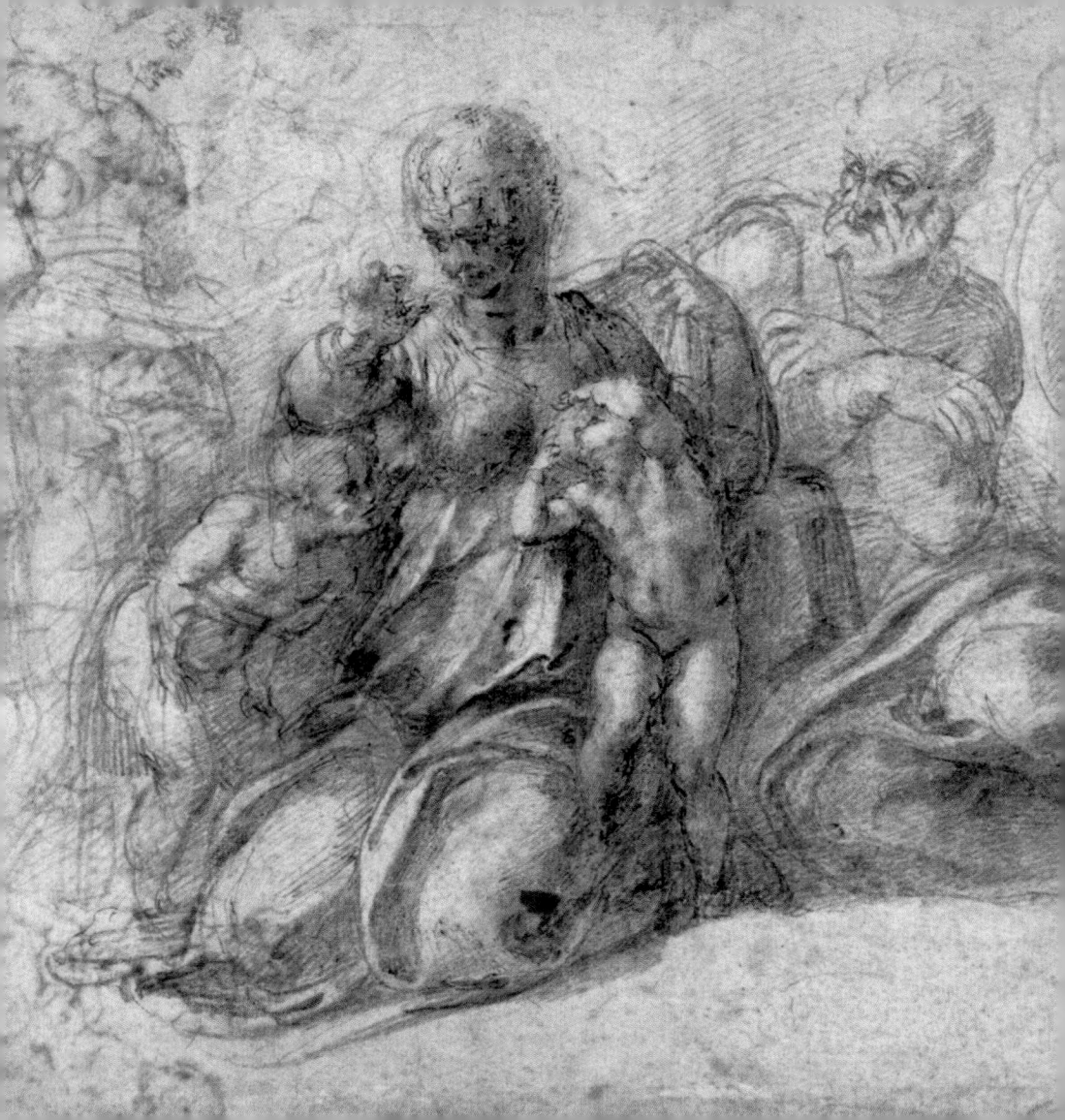

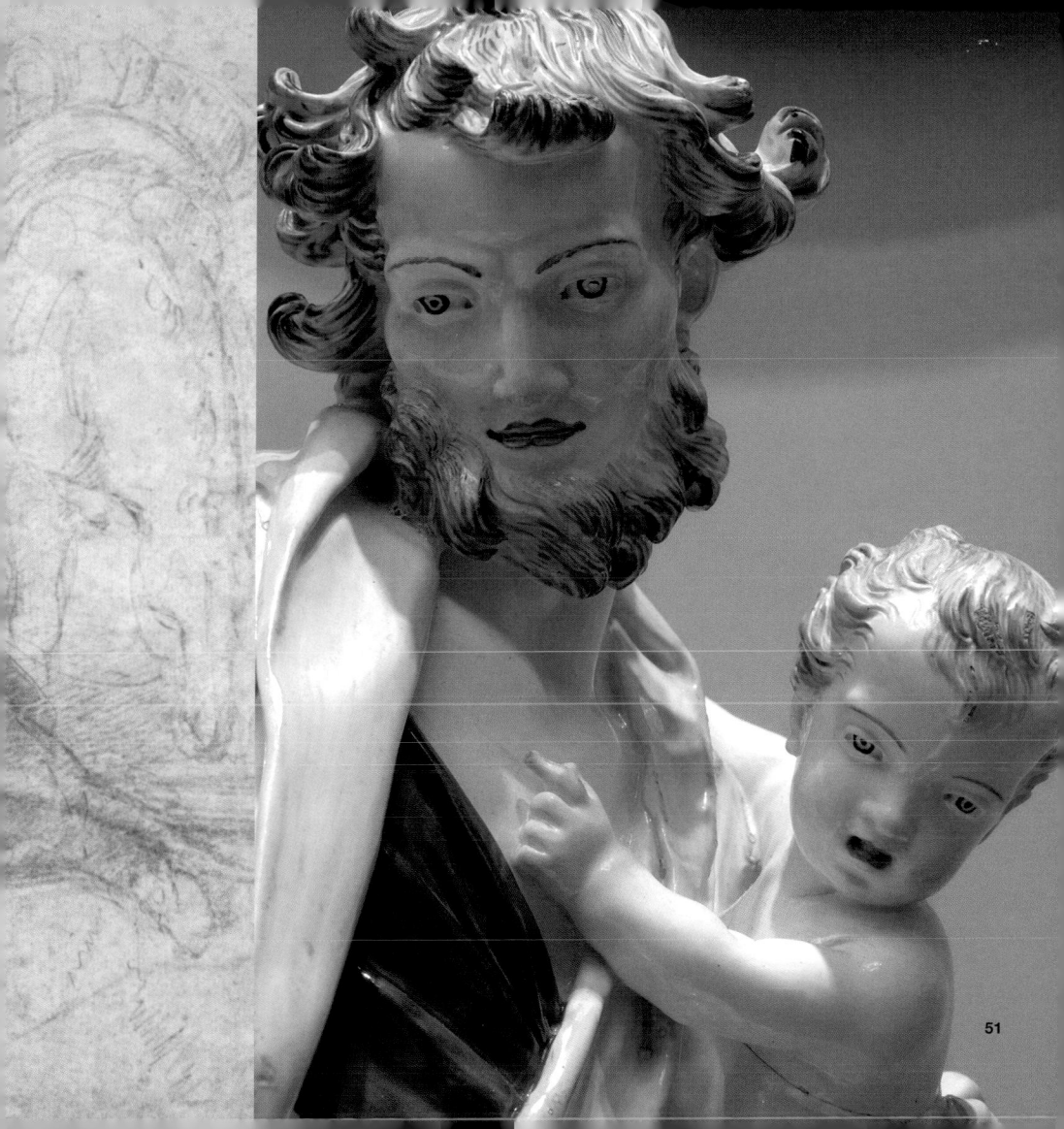

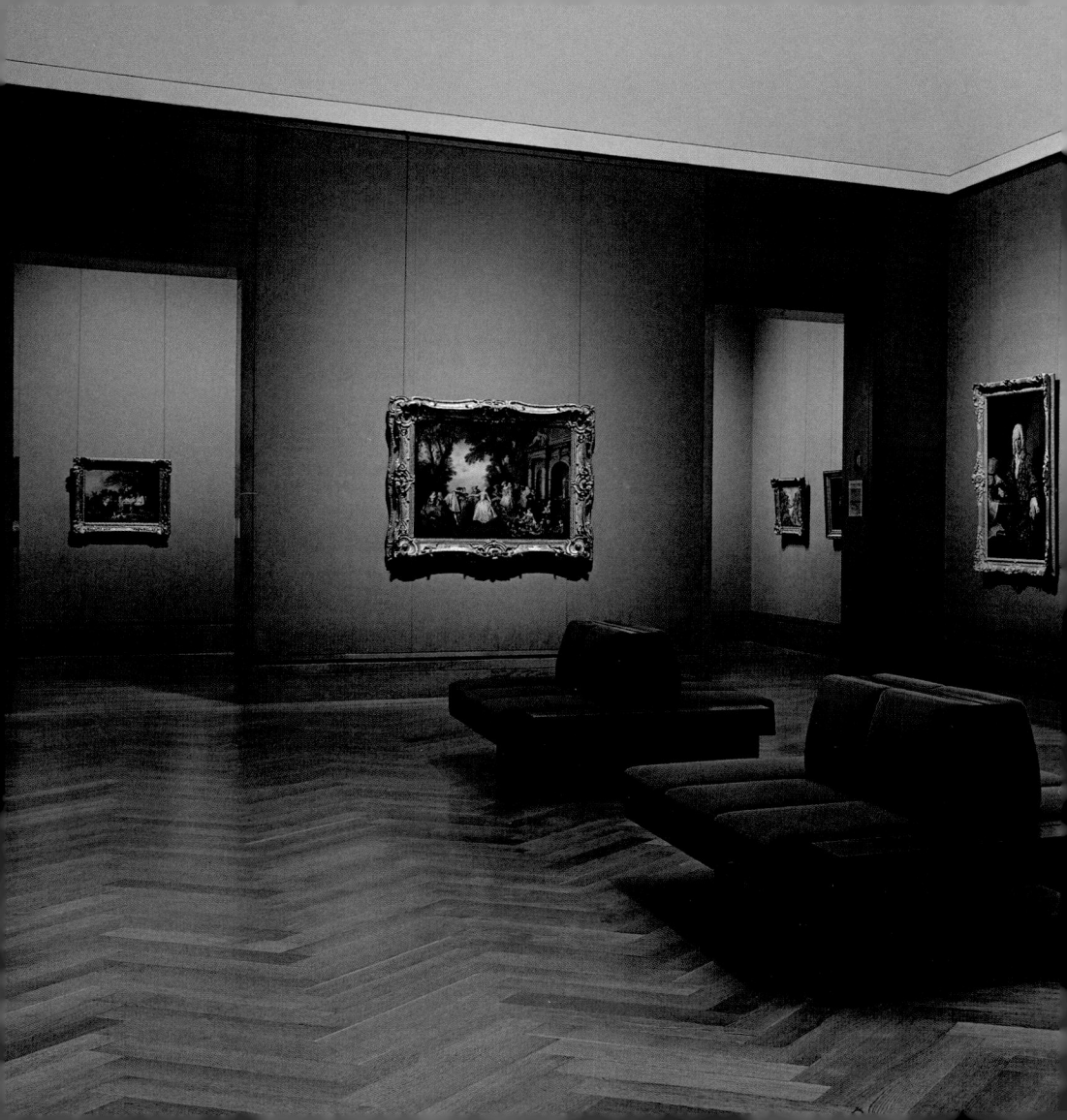

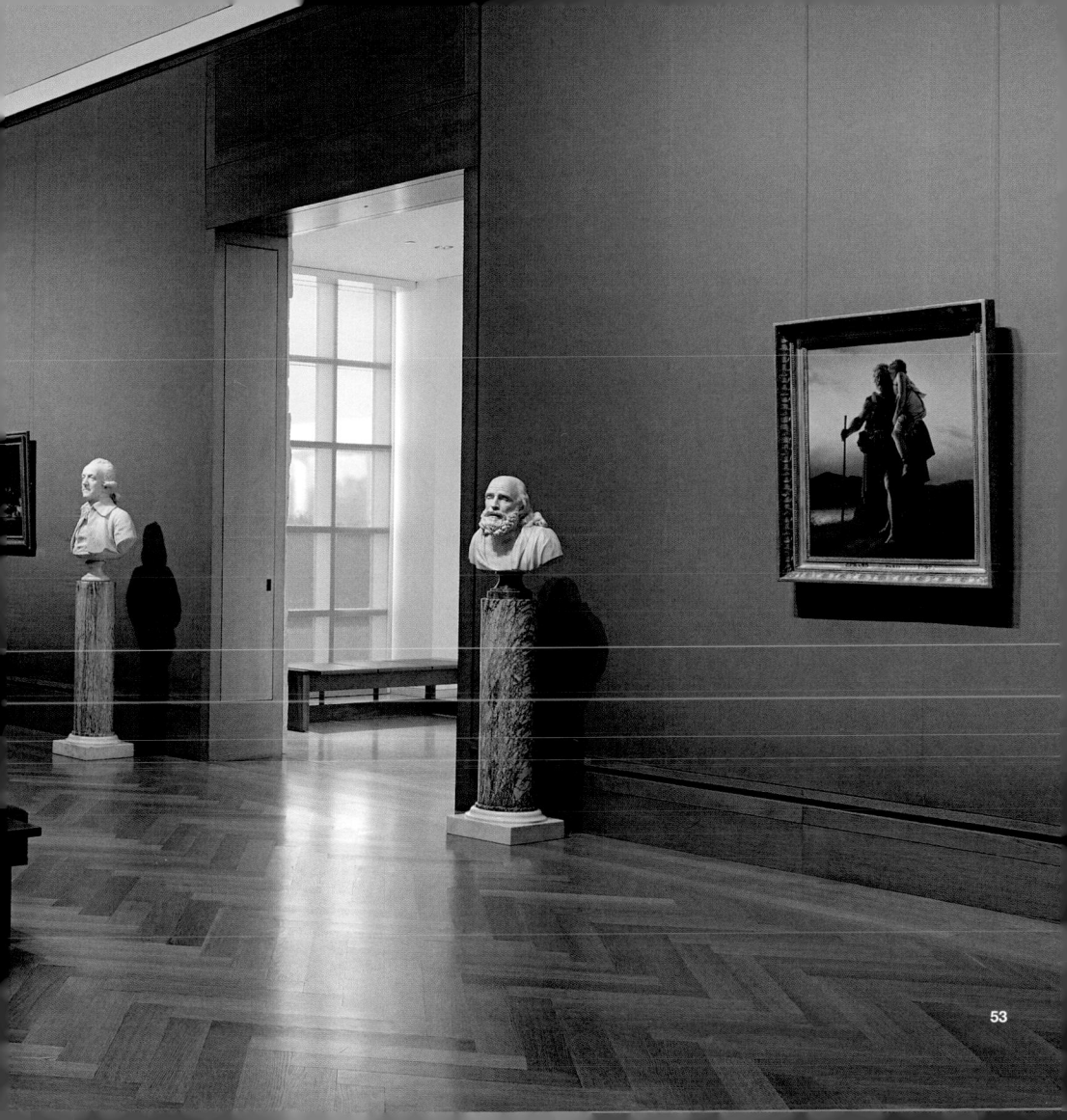

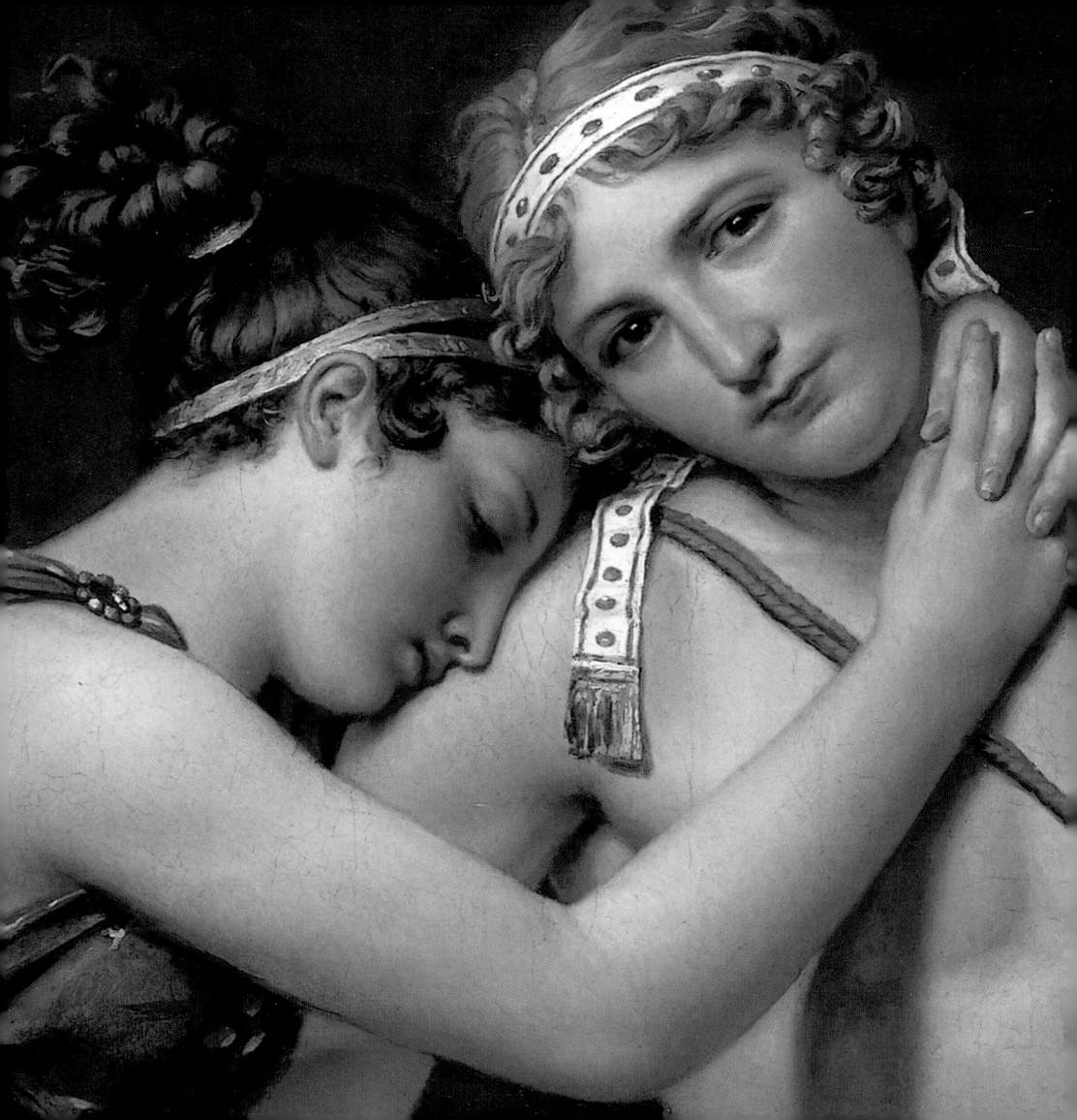

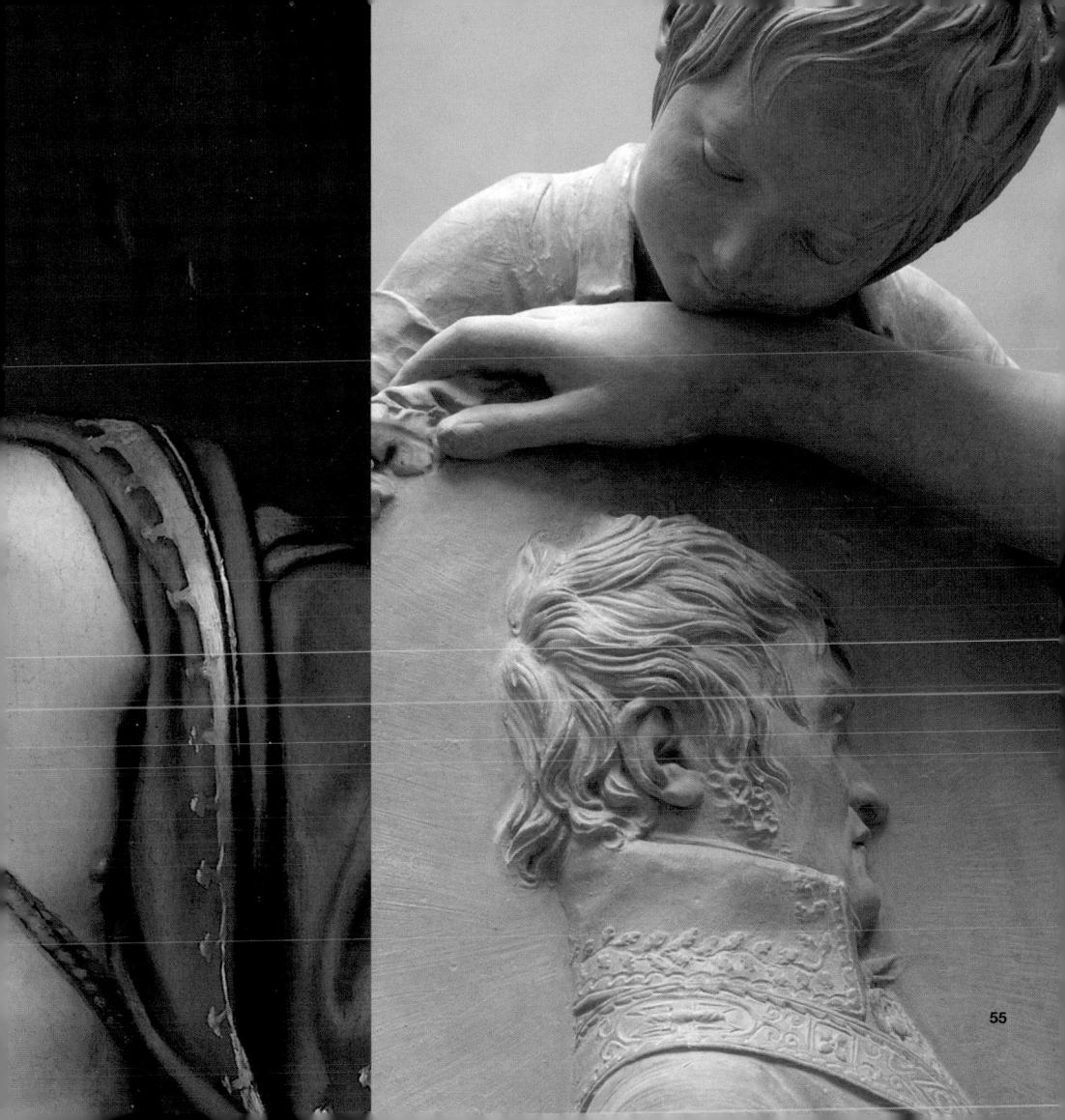

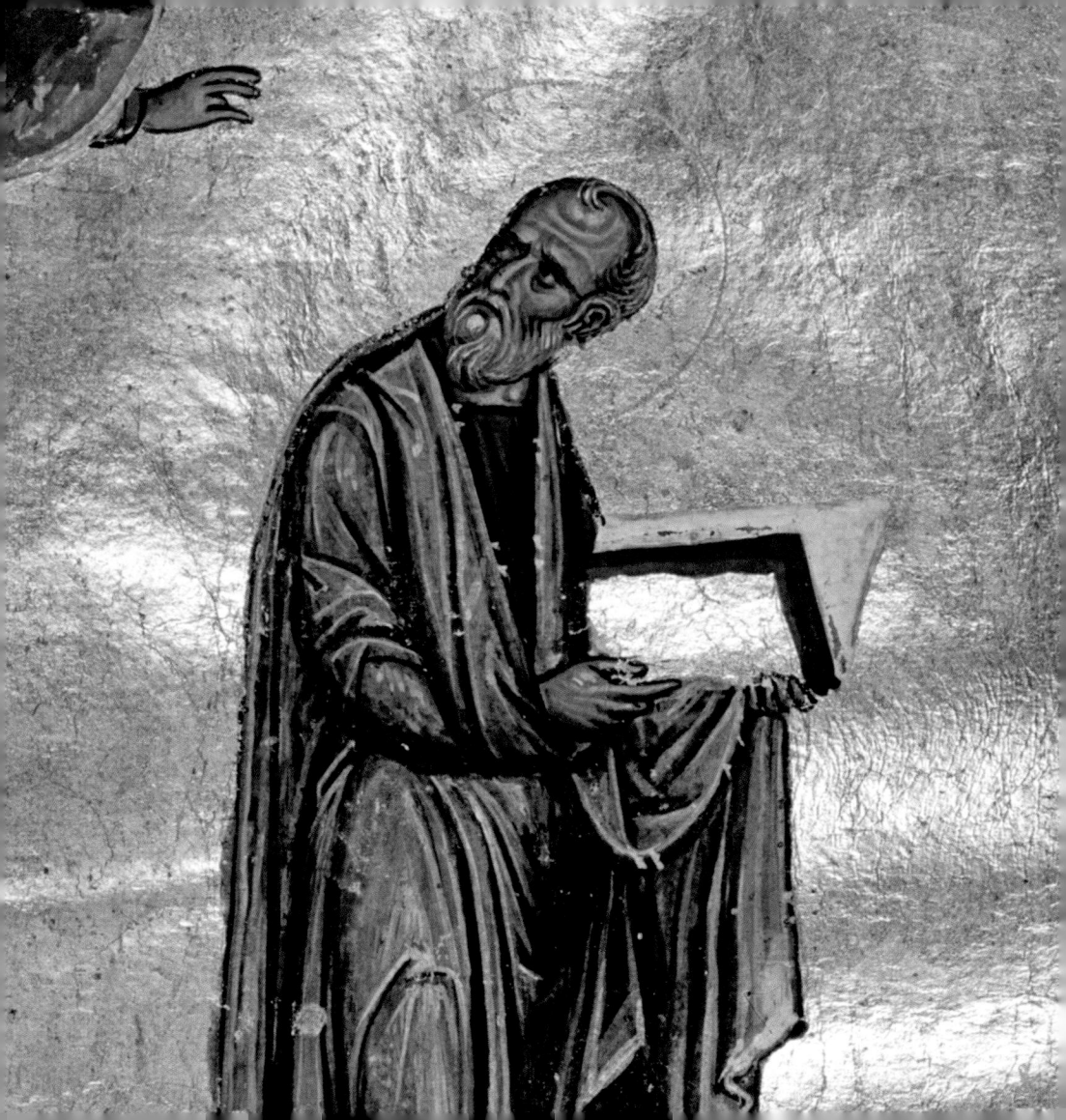

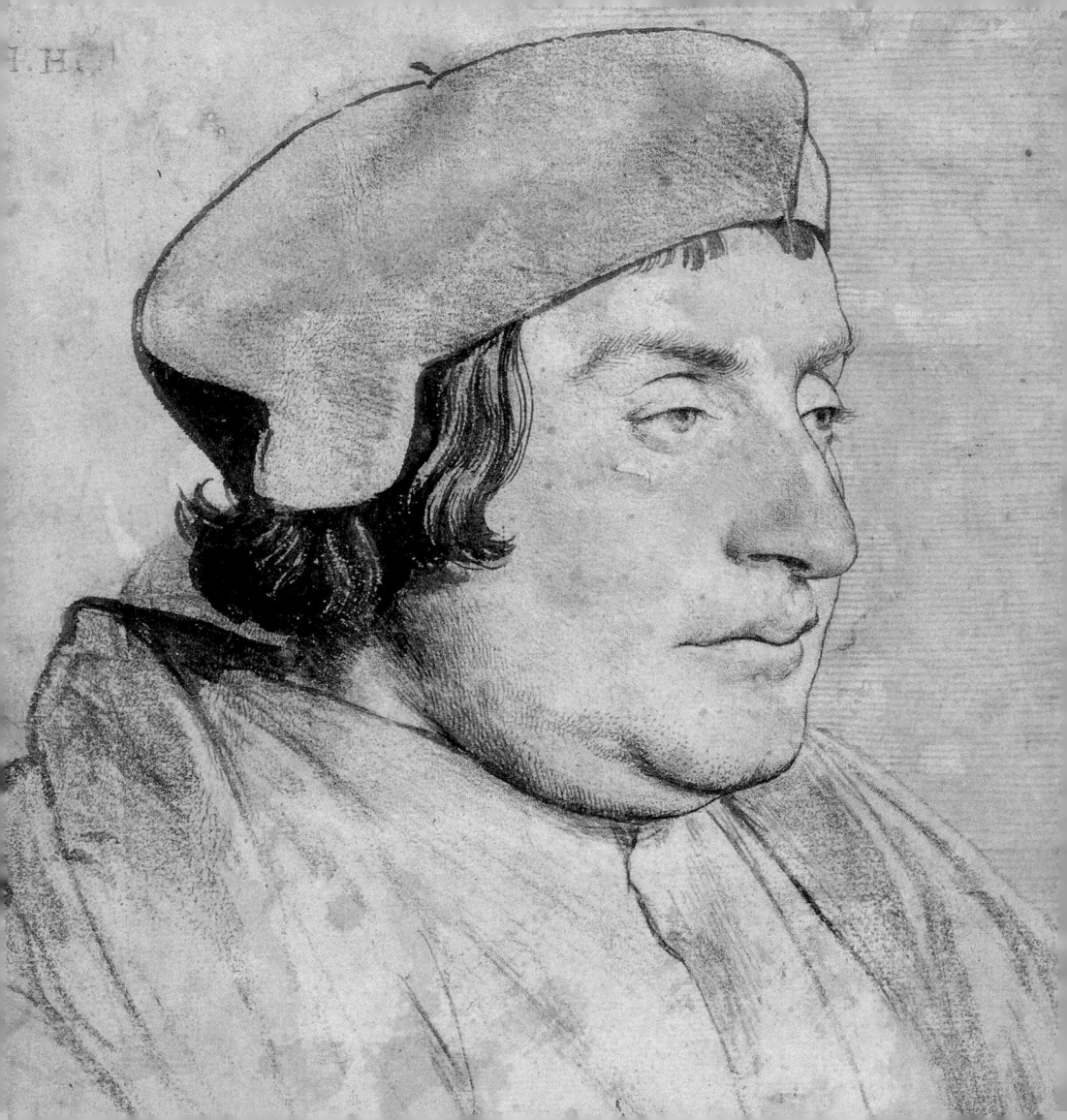
I.H.

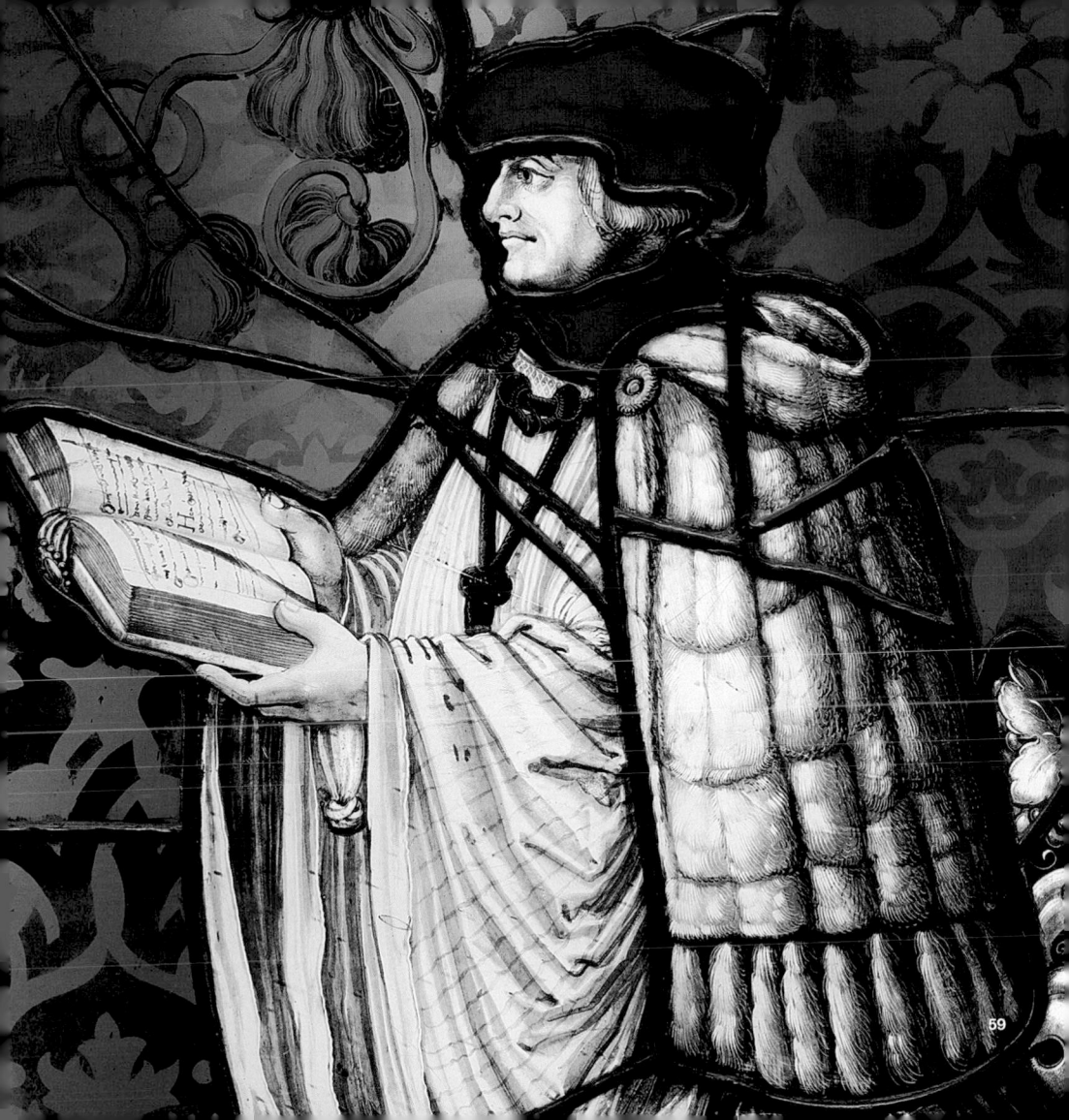

# ILLUSTRATIONS

**All images are details taken from the works of art listed below (numbers refer to pages). In most cases, the full work is illustrated, with commentary, in *The J. Paul Getty Museum: Handbook of the Collections* (7th edition, 2007)**

**Unless otherwise noted, all photographs were taken by the staff of the Imaging Services Department of the J. Paul Getty Museum and are © J. Paul Getty Trust**

**Front cover**
*Francisco de los Cobos y Molina*,
ca. 1530–32
JAN GOSSAERT (*called* Mabuse)
Netherlandish, ca. 1478–1532
Oil on panel
43.8 × 33.7 cm (17¼ × 13¼ in.)
88.PB.43

**Front flap**
*Medusa*, 1911
VINCENZO GEMITO
Italian, 1852–1929
Parcel-gilt silver
H: 23.5 cm (9¼ in.)
86.SE.528

**Back cover**
Long-case Musical Clock, ca. 1712
Attributed to
ALEXANDRE-JEAN OPPENORDT
French, 1639–1715
Veneered with brass and tortoise shell on oak carcass; bronze mounts, enameled metal
266.7 × 104.1 × 39.4 cm
(8 ft. 9 in. × 3 ft. 5 in. × 1 ft. 3¼ in.)
72.DB.40
[Detail of bronze mount]
Photo: Richard Ross

1 *The Portal of Rouen Cathedral in Morning Light*, 1894
CLAUDE MONET
French, 1840–1926
Oil on canvas
100 × 64.9 cm (39⅜ × 25⁹⁄₁₆ in.)
2001.33
Photo: Richard Ross

2 *Self-Portrait Playing the Lute*,
ca. 1940–44
AUGUST SANDER
German, 1876–1964
Gelatin silver print
22.5 × 16.8 cm (8⅞ × 6⅝ in.)
84.XM.126.68

3 Tapestry depicting musicians and dancers, 1690–1730
Beauvais Manufactory
French, founded in 1664
After designs by JEAN-BAPTISTE MONNOYER, 1636–1699
Wool and silk
316.87 × 521.97 cm
(10 ft. 4¾ in. × 17 ft. 1½ in.)
2003.4
Photo: Richard Ross

4 *The Vexed Man*, after 1770
FRANZ XAVER MESSERSCHMIDT
German, 1736–1783
Alabaster
2008.4

6-7 GALLERY OF EUROPEAN SCULPTURE FROM 1750 TO 1850
Photo: Richard Ross

from left to right:

6a *Bust of Felix Mendelssohn*, 1848
ERNST FRIEDRICH AUGUST RIETSCHEL
German, 1804–61
Marble
59.7 cm (23½ in.)
86.SA.543

6b *Allegorical Portrait of the van Risamburgh Family*, 1790
JOSEPH CHINARD
French, 1756–1813
Marble
H: 112.4 cm (44¼ in.)
94.SA.2

7a *Bust of Pseudo-Seneca* (after the antique), 1755–65
JOSEPH WILTON
British, 1722–1803
Marble
H: 61 cm (24 in.)
87.SA.111

7b *Bust of a Man* (after the antique), 1758
JOSEPH WILTON
British, 1722–1803
Marble
H: 59.7 cm (23½ in.)
87.SA.110